VICTOR JUHASZ
"Son of Moe"
(after Magritte)

PUBLISHER'S LETTER
BY MICHAEL GERBER

AN ORAL HISTORY OF THE FAKE MOON LANDING

Buzz Aldrin, astronaut: When Apollo 1 burned up, everything stopped so the engineers could figure out what happened. But the Russians were right on our tail, and by the time we got the green light, we were behind. Too far to catch up.

Bill Moyers, Presidential aide: October '67, we went down to NASA, to Houston, for a status report. I remember watching LBJ's face just fall. Calling it off was not on the table. *Never.* LBJ couldn't be seen as failing where Jack [Kennedy] had succeeded.

The room went quiet, then LBJ finally said, "Gentlemen, what we need here is a good ol' Texas Mindfuck."

Harry Rowan, President of RAND: I got a call from the White House: "Say someone wanted to fake a moon landing..." Our initial thought was Godard, but something told me, "Hold off." Then one of our younger associates was at a Hollywood party and saw some rough footage of *2001*. First thing Monday he comes in. "I know who can do it: Stanley Kubrick."

I was shocked. I mean, *Dr. Strangelove*? But he said the special effects were fantastic. I knew some illicit substances had been smoked at the party, so I asked to screen the material myself.

The next morning, I called Moyers.

Moyers: I remember thinking, "Von Braun is going to shit."

MICHAEL GERBER (@mgerber937) is Editor & Publisher of *The American Bystander*.

Wernher von Braun, inventor of the Saturn V: "Ja, ich habe mir eingeschissen."

Louis Blau, Kubrick's lawyer: At first, Stanley wasn't interested; he'd done space. "Get Blake Edwards."

But I pushed back. "Stan, you've got the entire U.S. space program over a barrel. You can name your price." He got this look in his eye. "You know, I've always wanted one of Napoleon's hats."

I'm not at liberty to say what we eventually settled on. A big number, in cash. But I don't think Stan took advantage.

Robert Evans, producer: Of course he took advantage! Wouldn't you? Stanley had ol' Uncle Sammy by the nuts and *squeezed*. How do you think he paid for that mansion in England? *Barry* fucking *Lyndon*? Oh yeah, Thackeray, that always packs 'em in.

Henry Michael, lawyer: Roughly 400,000 people worked on Apollo, and I handled the NDAs...Yes, I own this island.

Aldrin: When the word came down, we weren't just angry. I mean, Neil, Mike and I had been training *for years*. We'd blown up Apollo 1, just to jump in line.

Ha ha, just kidding.

[uncomfortable silence]

Neil Armstrong, astronaut: In the end, we were military men, and we followed orders. Plus, there was talk of Ford dealerships.

Michael Collins, astronaut: So NASA loaded the three of us onto a plane, plus all the gear, plus twenty or so I guess you'd call them "call girls with security clearance," and we headed to England.

Worst six months of my life. Girls were great, though. God bless you, Bubbles, wherever you are!

Aldrin: First time I saw Kubrick? Shepperton Studios; he came in to where Neil and I were getting makeup. Very quiet and nice; but *weird*. Bubbles described him as "the love child of Einstein and Zero Mostel," and I think that's right.

Armstrong: I'm always very neat, it's a Navy thing. I think Kubrick took one look at me and thought, "I hate this guy." At the secret premiere of the Moon Landing, I saw him wearing a $5,000 suit, and he still looked like a plate of mashed potatoes. With hair.

Margaret Tyzack, actress: There was no time, so Stanley used a lot of people from *2001*. I played a moon rock. Think I did it quite well!

There was a rumor that Sellers was playing the landing module. I was never sure about that—which goes to show Peter's immense range. I do remember Stanley wanted everybody on set to hold their breath, to give the scenes the right atmosphere. Or lack thereof.

Aldrin: Kubrick wore a football helmet when he was doing crane shots. They had to tie him to it, but also give him a knife, "in case I need to cut myself free from the wreckage."

That's when I realized, "This guy may not be carrying a full payload."

Moyers: I think that some part of Stanley wanted people to know. Every time I visited the set, and I visited several times to keep the President informed, I'd find a Coke bottle on the Moon, in the background. I'd give it to him, but it would always be there.

Ken Adams, art director:
God, the soda bottles! Drove me absolutely mad.

You know he wanted to make the whole film some sort of barmy commentary on Austerlitz? I remember saying, "Stan, don't mess about. This is the United States government, they have bloody *guns*."

Aldrin: He and I used to play "chess" as they were setting up in the mornings. I put it in quotes because—people say Kubrick was a chess fanatic, but that's just Hollywood. When we started to play he kept shouting, "King me!" Holy shit. This guy had been playing checkers, with chess pieces, for years. And nobody had told him! So *I* told him. "Stanley, that's not how you play chess." He didn't believe me.

Then an assistant brought him a book, and he read it, silently. Then he just went apeshit, throwing all the pieces around. We thought they'd all been picked up, but one of them landed on set. Someone spotted it in dailies, and we lost two weeks of work.

Moyers: He had this whole cockamamie narration. You'd see the Moon, then hear: "The year is 1805. The place, Czechoslovakia…" It just didn't work. Plus it was in his voice, with that heavy Bronx accent. "…da plainz a' Czechoslovakia…" We were all saying, "Stanley, people can't know it's you." We kept explaining that this was a secret, that we were trying to hide it, and I don't think Kubrick ever understood that.

Evans: Of course he understood! He just didn't give a shit.

Wendy Carlos, composer:
With Stanley it was always like, "Drop everything and help me!"

"Okay. What do you want?"

"*A robot fucking God.*"

Later, those tapes were lost in a fire, which I'm grateful for.

Aldrin: Finally the big day comes, Neil's Giant Step.

Armstrong: I can't talk about it.

Aldrin: He had to do 102 takes. Neil'd step on the moon, and Kubrick would come craning down: "No! Go again!"

Neil was never a drinker, but he started now. He was in pretty bad shape, weaving around, trying to plant the flag and stabbing himself in the leg. Sellers made a joke, and Neil busted him in the jaw, and suddenly we had no LEM.

Collins: I think Kubrick was torturing him. He called Neil "Space Goy."

Aldrin: After about two weeks, Neil snapped. He tore off his suit and ran out screaming. The police picked him up four miles away in Chertsey Meads.

JOE CIARDIELLO

Neil was naked, and totally out of his head. "*One* small step…one *small* step…one small *step*."

Blau: Stanley did what any director would do. He cut all Neil's scenes, and replaced him with Peter Sellers.

Sellers played all the astronauts. One was Indian.

Moyers: Project Mindfuck was supposed to end on January 1, 1968. We needed thirty minutes of footage for Cronkite: Landing, stepping, collecting, some human interest B-roll, done.

So there we are in October, billions over budget, with thirty-three hours of footage. Twenty thousand extras in Napoleonic uniforms are rolling around Czechoslovakia, which was still behind the Iron Curtain by the way. The President is going absolutely nuts, and Kubrick's still in the editing suite, cutting and re-cutting. NASA calls, and he puts them off; then he stops answering at all. Finally LBJ's sending Phantoms to strafe his house. He had to get permission from the Queen. She saw a little of the film and said, "1,000% behind you."

LBJ got so frustrated he just quit. That's why he didn't run for President again. Vietnam was nothing compared to Stanley Kubrick. But there was one thing Kubrick didn't count on: Richard Nixon was crazier than he was.

H.R. Haldeman, Nixon aide:
The moment Nixon heard about it, he shut everything down.

"Kubrick—that's a *Jew* name, right?"

Aldrin: Suddenly, we were going up again. It was utter bedlam—they were literally using parts from lawnmowers.

Armstrong: I didn't care. If we died, at least it would be over in one take.

Clark Clifford, LBJ aide
Lyndon was too angry, so I screened it. That film was… criminal.

Have you ever seen *Magical Mystery Tour*? It was like that, but without the Beatles.

LBJ wanted to nuke him. We tried to lure Kubrick to an isolated atoll, but couldn't get him to fly.

Evans: Stanley had final cut, so what could the government do? I've dealt with Hollywood shysters, and trust me: it was cheaper to just go to the moon.

Armstrong: I was in therapy for years. You know, everybody thinks I said, "One small step for man…" but if you listen closely, that's Stanley's voice. They dubbed it from his V.O. It's the only part of his crappy movie that made it.

…What did I really say?

[Armstrong smiles.]

"FUCK YOU STANLEY KUBRICK!"

TABLE OF CONTENTS

The AMERICAN BYSTANDER
#16 • Vol. 4, No. 4 • September 2020

TRACEY BERGLUND

EDITOR & PUBLISHER Michael Gerber
HEAD WRITER Brian McConnachie
SENIOR EDITOR Alan Goldberg
ORACLE Steve Young
STAFF LIAR P.S. Mueller
INTREPID TRAVELER Mike Reiss
EAGLE EYES Patrick L. Kennedy
AGENTS OF THE SECOND BYSTANDER INTERNATIONAL
Eve Alintuck, Craig Boreth, Joey Green, Matt Kowalick, Neil Mitchell, Maxwell Ziegler
MANAGING EDITOR EMERITA
Jennifer Finney Boylan
WARTIME CONSIGLIERA
Kate Powers
CONTRIBUTORS
Lucas Adams, Melissa Balmain, Ron Barrett, Tracey Berglund, Barry Blitt, George Booth, M.K. Brown, Adam Chase, Joe Ciardiello, Danielle Deschenes, Ben Doyle, Larry Doyle, Marques Duggans, Bob Eckstein, Peter Elwell, Randall Enos, Hannah Ferguson, Emily Flake, Chris Galletta, Gregory Gerber, Rick Geary, Sam Gross, Lance Hansen, Jake Houston, Tim Hunt, Sarah Hutto, Victor Juhasz, Ben Kawaller, Paul Karasik, Lars Kenseth, Joe Keohane, Harrison Scott Key, John Klossner, Jeff Kulik, Mary Lawton, Robert McGee, Drew Panckeri, Matt Percival, Michael Pershan, Nathan Place, Jonathan Plotkin, Denise Reiss, John Reynolds, Jason Roeder, Ellis Rosen, Mike Sacks, Tim Sniffen, Nick Spooner, Mick Stevens, Ed Subitzky, B.A. Van Sise, Dalton Vaughn, Shannon Wheeler, D. Watson, and Steve Young.

DEPARTMENTS
Frontispiece: "Son of Moe" **by Victor Juhasz** 1
Publisher's Letter **by Michael Gerber** 2
The Man and the Can **by Ron Barrett** 76

GALLIMAUFRY
Melissa Balmain, Damask Pugh, Tim Sniffen, Barry Blitt, Ben Doyle, Adam Chase, Hannah Ferguson, Nick Spooner, Nathan Place, Robert McGee, Ellis Rosen, Jeff Kulik, Mary Lawton, Joe Keohane, Jake Houston, Tim Hunt.

SHORT STUFF
Marooned! **by D. Watson** 8
Spotlight **by Shannon Wheeler** 10
Subject: Re: Some Very Serious Issues
  by Michael Pershan 23
Back in the Day **by Steve Young** 24
We Are Making Changes **by Larry Doyle** 26
I Have Now Perfected My Signature Dish: Lemon Pasta
  by Bob Eckstein 28
I Respond to Famous Old Man Writers Trying to Chat Me Up
  At a Party **by Sarah Hutto** 30
Give Yourself a Pat on the Mind! **by Lars Kenseth** 32

.... ◆ ....

Katie Callaghan, Lanky Bareikis, Jon Schwarz, Karen Backus, Alleen Schultz, Gray & Bernstein, Joe Lopez, Ivanhoe & Gumenick, Greg & Trish Gerber, thank ya.
NAMEPLATES BY Mark Simonson
ISSUE CREATED BY Michael Gerber

Vol. 4, No. 4. ©2020 Good Cheer LLC, all rights reserved. Proudly produced in sunny Santa Monica, California, USA.

CELADON BOOKS

"BOYLAN'S WRY WIT, WICKED SENSE OF HUMOR, AND UNIQUE WAY OF TURNING PHRASES SHINE THROUGH..."
~KIRKUS REVIEWS

GOOD BOY
MY LIFE IN SEVEN DOGS

A NEW MEMOIR BY JENNIFER FINNEY BOYLAN, *NEW YORK TIMES* BESTSELLING AUTHOR OF *SHE'S NOT THERE: A LIFE IN TWO GENDERS*

"*Good Boy* is a warm, funny, instantly engaging testament to the power of love—canine and human—to ease us through life's radical transitions. And I say that as a cat person!"

~JENNIFER EGAN
Winner of the Pulitzer Prize and author of *A Visit from the Goon Squad* and *Manhattan Beach*

"Dogs help us understand ourselves: who we are, who we've been. They teach us what it means to love, and to be loved. They bear witness to our joys and sorrows; they lick the tears from our faces. And when our backs are turned, they steal a whole roasted chicken off the supper table."

~JENNIFER FINNEY BOYLAN

ON SALE APRIL 21, 2020 PRE-ORDER NOW

CELADONBOOKS.COM/BOOKSHOP

FEATURES

Welcome to Woodmont College *by Jason Roeder & Mike Sacks*	35
Naked Homosexual Desert Caper *by Ben Kawaller*	46
Sheriff Tick *by Lucas Adams*	52
Ike of the Foolsguard *by Chris Galletta*	54
Real Boy's Life *by Michael Gerber*	58
The Old Man With No Pants *by Harrison Scott Key*	64
What They're Thinking *by Ed Subitzky*	68

OUR BACK PAGES

Notes From a Small Planet *by Rick Geary*	71
What Am I Doing Here? *by Mike Reiss*	73
P.S. Mueller Thinks Like This *by P.S. Mueller*	75

CARTOONS & ILLUSTRATIONS BY

Emily Flake, Victor Juhasz, Joe Ciardiello, Tracey Berglund, George Booth, Barry Blitt, Sam Gross, D. Watson, Shannon Wheeler, Hannah Ferguson, Nick Spooner, Nathan Place, Ellis Rosen, Mary Lawton, Tim Hunt, Jonathan Plotkin, Dalton Vaughn, Bob Eckstein, Lance Hansen, Lars Kenseth, Danielle Deschenes, Marques Duggans, Mick Stevens, John Klossner, Lucas Adams, Peter Elwell, Matt Percival, Gregory Gerber, M.K. Brown, John Reynolds, Paul Karasik, B.A. Van Sise, Drew Panckeri, Ed Subitzky, Rick Geary, Denise Reiss, P.S. Mueller, and Ron Barrett.

.... ◆ ....

Sam's Spot

COVER

If one had to sum up the dreadful unSummer of '20, it would be hard to top **EMILY FLAKE**'s cover. Is she avoiding COVID? Marauding Feds? Trumpy caravans? Oh well, we'll try again next year.

ACKNOWLEDGMENTS

All material is ©2020 its creators, all rights reserved; please do not reproduce/distribute it without written consent of the creators and *Bystander*. For the Woodmont College parody, here are the image credits: man vomiting ©Yuri_Arcurs/iStock.com; man wearing inflatable penis costume (ID 116002140) ©Arts1961/Dreamstime.com, group of students ©JP WALLET, and college campus ©Wangkun Jia; all other images courtesy of Shutterstock.com: page 36 © FGC; page 40 © Ysbrand Cosijn; page 41 (top) © Andrey Arkusha; page 41 (bottom) © Wong Yu Liang; page 43 © Istvan Csak; page 10 school building doodle © IrynMerry; page 10 foam finger © goir; page 10 (bottom) © VDB Photos; page 11 © DGIM studio. Campus map by D. Watson. "The Old Man With No Pants" originally appeared in *The Oxford American*.

.... ◆ ....

THE AMERICAN BYSTANDER, *Vol. 4, No. 4*, (978-0-578-66568-9). Publishes ~5x/year. ©2020 by Good Cheer LLC. No part of this magazine can be reproduced, in whole or in part, by any means, without the written permission of the Publisher. For this and other queries, email *Publisher@americanbystander.org*, or write: Michael Gerber, Publisher, *The American Bystander*, 1122 Sixth St., #403, Santa Monica, CA 90403. **Subscribe at www.patreon.com/bystander**. Other info can be found at www.americanbystander.org.

THE MARGARET CHO

EARIOS

ICONIC COMEDIAN MARGARET CHO TALKS WITH PEOPLE YOU KNOW, AND PEOPLE YOU SHOULD KNOW.

  acast

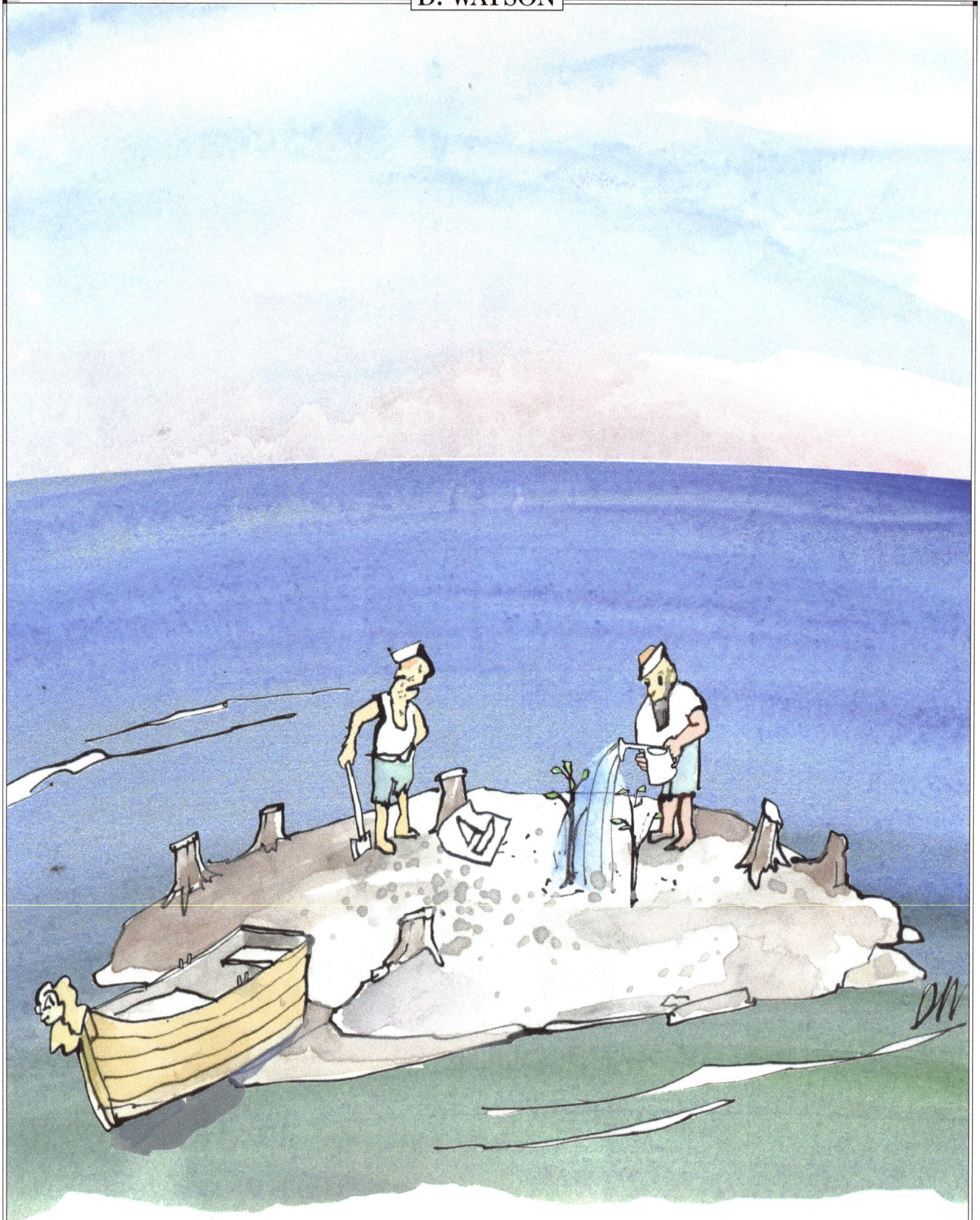

"Well, it's a plan."

SIX OF THE BEST
BY SHANNON WHEELER
SPOTLIGHT
The only way to win is not to play.

"Where do you see yourself in two billion years?"

"I want a cat."

"Pavlov, stop with the bell ringing already."

"Just tell us who's winning."

"I'm sick of nostalgia for things that were crappy to begin with."

SHANNON WHEELER *(@MuchCoffee) is the creator of* **Too Much Coffee Man**. *His latest book,* **The Mueller Report: Graphic Novel**, *is available on Kindle September 16.*

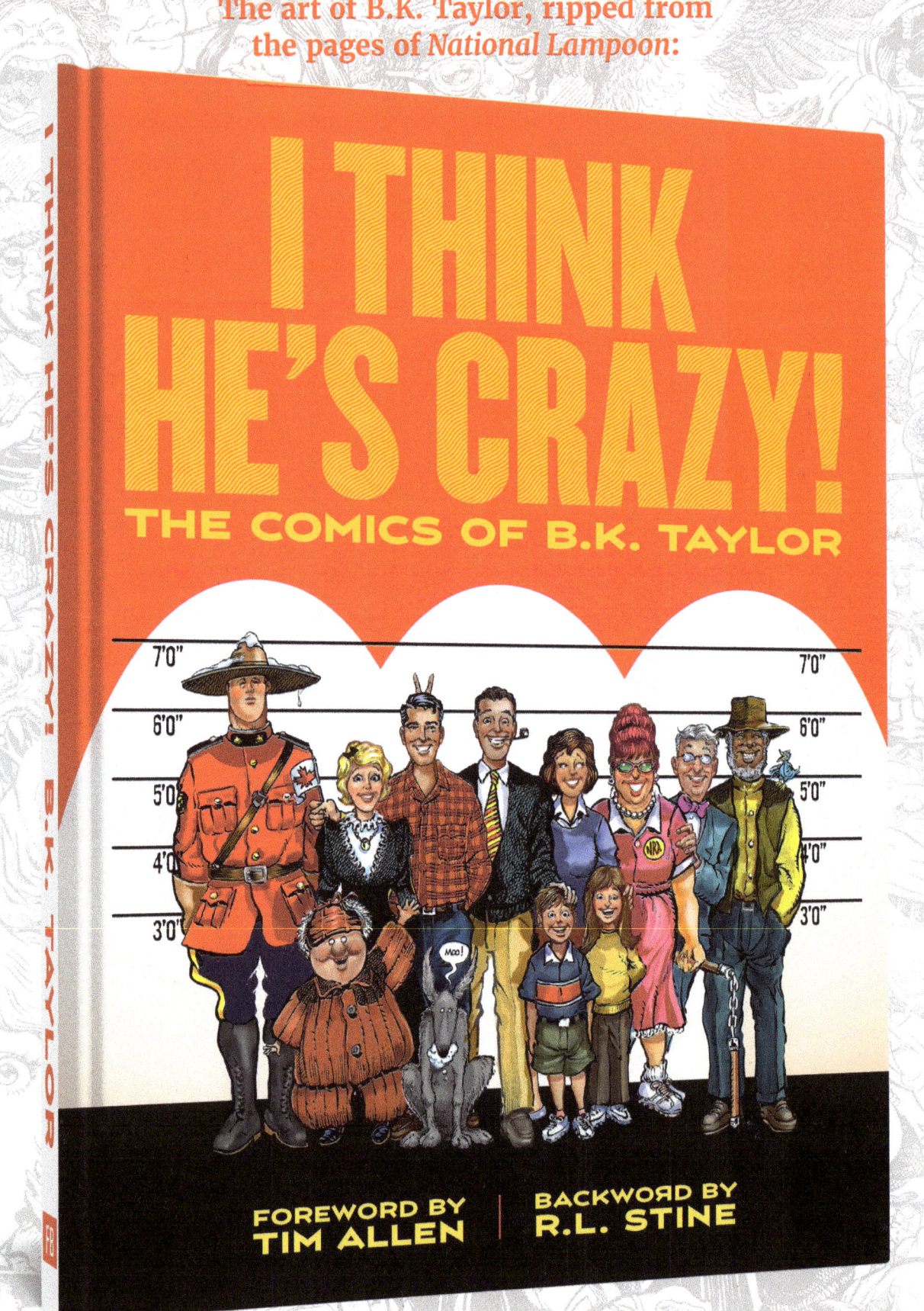

Gallimaufry

Before
My stomach feels sick
at the size of her stick.

During
Anxiety grows
as she roots in my nose.

After
Forget all the minuses:
I've now got clean sinuses.

—**Melissa Balmain**

INTRODUCING MY NEW ASSISTANT, WHO IS ABSOLUTELY NOT MY TODDLER IN A MOUSTACHE AND FEDORA.

Morning, everybody!

Listen, before we start today's Zoom, I just wanted to apologize for yesterday. Right before we got on, my usual sitter tested positive—thanks, I'm sure we'll be fine—and then, as I was listening to Caryl's truly brilliant analysis of the phone records, my three-year-old's daycare sent a text saying everyone was being sent home, and they'll be remote-only until Easter.

Apologies for blowing out any laptop speakers. And sorry again, Caryl. Your new bangs look great. I was just…I wasn't at my best.

Now, this morning, I find out that installing a full-time nanny in my basement violates a whole bunch of human trafficking laws. What are we supposed to do? Can you believe this shit?

Luckily, my work-life issues are behind me. Millstone and Associates, allow me to introduce my new assistant, Giorgio. He's the product of an exhaustive six-month hiring process and not, I assure you, the country's total fuckup that leaves people with motherfucking full-time jobs no place to stick their motherfucking kids.

No, I'm not mad at you, Giorgio, I'm mad at society. Take the blanket off your head and wave to your new colleagues, like I showed you.

Giorgio joins us from his home office that looks a hell of a lot like my laundry room but isn't. He signed his very generous offer letter this morning and is beyond thrilled to join the Millstone team—he hopes you'll be patient with his thick Venetian accent, which may sound to the untrained ear like the gibberish of a common toddler. I myself find it charming, and encourage anyone who feels differently to take a good, hard look at their own internalized xenophobia.

As you can see from the full, billowing lines of his blazer—that's how they wear 'em in Venice, roomy—Giorgio brings a real sense of Tom Ford elegance, balanced with enough humor to leave some—what is it? Bananas?—smeared across his forehead.

Please know that Giorgio's door is always open. Don't be surprised if you get "No-no-no-no-NOOOOOOO!" as an answer to any question; just try again in a robot voice. Everything is robots right now with him.

Right, buddy? Robot Boss says, you're slouching out of frame! Beep beep boop boop! Okay, enough fucking around. Let's get into the evidence for the Barrett defense.

This morning, we got the slides back from the lab—looks like any "confusion" over those being exit wounds—*no, Giorgio, we leave Mr. Goldfish in his bowl. Sure, put some crayons in there with him, why the hell not.*

As I was saying, the revised coroner's report couldn't be better for us. The weapon which made the wounds was definitely serrated, which accounts for the copious amounts of—*GIORGIO! Good robots keep their hands out of the bowl! Thanks, buddy.*

In addition to the wounds and the neuro-toxicology, which we're still waiting on, and the arcing pattern of the massive electrical discharge, there's the ATM camera footage. That's key, so it's all hands on deck. Half of you, work on

SELF-HELP BOOKS AS WRITTEN BY MY MOTHER

by Ben Doyle & Adam Chase

that—go frame by frame. The killer is on that footage. The other half, I need you teaching my assistant the rest of the alphabet. Think of it as *Giorgio v. Everything Past M*. Bring in flash cards, songs, whatever it takes. Loop me in to consult on a killer robot voice.

Some of you might be thinking, "Stu, is this the time for a new assistant? The lives of seven defendants—we fuck this up, the whole family gets lethal injection."

Believe me, this is the only way. We can't afford more days like yesterday—Caryl, I see you nodding, you're not wrong. Plus, Esmeralda's infected ass could be out for weeks, Easter is a million fucking years away, and the chance of things going back to normal before then is the same as the Barrett family seeing next Christmas.

Great, now I've done it. *Giorgio, come on, the Barrett family is gonna be fine. Don't make me mute you—HEY, ROBOTS DON'T CRY THEIR FIRST DAY ON THE JOB, BEEP BEEP BOOP. There you go, sure, have some bananas from your forehead, lay your head on the desk—you've earned it.*

That's how it's done, fuckers! Now let's get to work.

—*Tim Sniffen*

SATAN TALKS TO HIS THERAPIST.

I've had four perfect years planned out for *ages*:

Split families up and stick the brats in cages;
dump cherished friendships in a flaming pool;
give power only to the dumb or cruel
and money just to those who have too much.

Let wholesome standards wither at my touch;
get better at exterminating birds
and swapping forests out for cattle herds;
befoul each breath of air and gulp of water.

Grant every mother, girlfriend, wife or daughter
the same respect as parasitic worms;
rouse bigots (in amusing coded terms)
while keeping them supplied with Colts and Glocks.

Where there's a henhouse, guard it with a Fox;
spawn loopholes, larceny and legalese;
and best of all, when there's a new disease,

"Heavens no, we don't vaccinate. Why?"

make sure fantastic numbers will be killed…

And yet (life isn't fair!) I'm unfulfilled.
Each time I try to carry out a plan,
I'm beaten to it by that blasted *man*.
Each yummy lie I long to spread? He's spread it.

At least some people give me all the credit.

—Melissa Balmain

INT. JERRY'S APARTMENT – DAY

GEORGE enters. JERRY is in the kitchen, eating cereal.
GEORGE: Well, it's all over, Jerry.
JERRY: The date didn't go well?
GEORGE: It started off fine. A walk in the park. A nice conversation. And then we tried to go in a store and she refused to wear a mask.
JERRY: She refused to wear a mask?
GEORGE: Refused to wear a mask.
JERRY: She's a no-masker?
GEORGE: A no-masker, Jerry!
George falls to his knees, raises his arms and yells. KRAMER bursts through the door, looks at George, and then at Jerry.
KRAMER: Date with a no-masker?

Jerry raises his cereal spoon in affirmation.

............◆............

INT. JERRY'S APARTMENT - DAY
ELAINE sits on the sofa. Jerry is in the kitchen, eating cereal.

ELAINE: So, what's the big deal? Just because he has to quarantine doesn't mean we can't yada yada yada online.
JERRY: That's a big step.
ELAINE: Is it though? I mean if I've seen it before, what's the big deal?
JERRY: Well, IT doesn't photograph well.
ELAINE: It doesn't.
JERRY: IT certainly does not.
ELAINE: But you guys send them around all the time.
JERRY: That's different. That's the golden rule.
ELAINE: Golden rule?
JERRY: Treating others the way we'd like to be treated.
ELAINE: So you think I should…

—*Illustrations by Hannah Ferguson*

Kramer crashes through the door.

KRAMER: What are we talking about?
ELAINE: The golden rule.
KRAMER: Oh ho, that doesn't photograph well.

Jerry raises his cereal spoon in affirmation.

.... ◆ ....

INT. JERRY'S APARTMENT - DAY
George enters from the bathroom. Jerry is in the kitchen, eating cereal.

GEORGE: What happened to your bathroom scale?
JERRY: I got rid of it.
GEORGE: Got rid of it?
JERRY: Threw it out.
GEORGE: Broken?
JERRY: Didn't need it.
GEORGE: What do you have going on behind that counter?
JERRY: Nothing. A few corona-kilos.
GEORGE: You mean pounds.
JERRY: 'Pounds' is aggressive. I prefer kilos.
There's a knock on the door.
JERRY: Come in.

NEWMAN *enters.*

NEWMAN: Jerry.
JERRY: Newman.
NEWMAN: Kramer wants to know if you could...
Newman tilts his head, looking behind Jerry's counter.
NEWMAN: Hiding a few corona kilos, Jerry?

Jerry lifts his cereal spoon in affirmation.

—Robert McGee

STAYIN' ALIVE.

Raymond slurped his lukewarm instant coffee and grimaced.

"At least we got coffee," Dave said. "Til it runs out."

"This ain't coffee."

Dave picked up the glass canister and turned it so Raymond could see. "Look at this guy, grinning like an idiot. He's damn happy. He's grateful."

Brett the intern stood in the corner, watching. Raymond put his hand on Brett's shoulder.

"Don't listen to Dave. He still has dreams of the old ways. He'll fill you with false hope."

"For crying out loud, Raymond! Give the kid a break!"

Raymond ignored his boss. Such distinctions meant less than nothing, now. "C'mon kid."

They walked down the long office hallway, Raymond's arm around the intern the whole time.

"Hell of a thing, what happened. Shutdown happens your first week on the job."

The intern didn't say anything. He never said anything.

"I never thought it would happen," Raymond said, "especially not in the middle of a workday. I thought they'd at least send us home first. But they didn't." Raymond leaned in, and the kid smelled his Sanka-breath. "Bet you wish you'd called in sick!"

The intern looked inside the open office doors as they walked by, offices that had slowly become ersatz studio apartments—complete with webs of laundry hanging from the ceiling, and half-eaten bags of vending machine chips strewn on the carpet.

"I never got to show you around," Raymond said. "Well, now we got time. Nothing but time."

The intern nodded, rubbing his stubble. He hadn't showered in a week and was subsisting on nothing but rationed candy bars.

They stopped at an office. "This here's Martha. She's the one you hear every night around five. Used to be quitting time. Hey, Martha, what was that you sang for us last night?"

"'Controversy.' Tonight, I'm trying to write down all the lyrics I can remember from 'Get Into The Groove.'"

Raymond raised his mug in salute, then they walked on. "When the internet went out, I realized something. Do you know what I realized, Brett? Every day, in a million little ways, the internet had started to replace our memory." Raymond squeezed the intern's shoulders for emphasis. Then he paused to take a mouthful of Sanka.

"UGH. If nothing else, not having the internet has made us, what you call, reformulate all the stuff in our heads that we like. You know? No choice but to commit it all to memory."

They kept walking, and Raymond kept pontificating. "You don't know what it was like. Your generation always had the internet. But there was a whole world before it. Look out."

"HELLLOOOO Mom!"

Raymond sharply kicked a binder carelessly dropped in the hall. "Things, Brett, were mysterious. When you didn't know something, and it wasn't in the ol' Funk & Wagnalls—that's an encyclopedia—you were out of luck. Maybe you'd run into someone who knew it, or maybe you just never were gonna find out. You had to accept it, and make more room in the old noggin for the stuff you liked.

"People who were good at trivia were prized. Champions. If you knew the real lyrics to 'Louie, Louie,' then you were the king in the land of the blind, my friend."

"'Louie, Louie?'"

"Old song. We'll get Martha to sing it. Then," Raymond said, "POW. Anybody could look up anything at the drop of a hat. Your brain became like your tonsils. Useless, expendable. Not anymore!"

They reached the end of the hall, and stood in the doorway of a half-lit conference room. Inside, a wavy-haired man sat at the head of a long table. In each chair, sat a disheveled office worker, paying rapt attention.

"…That day, when he approached the door, he knocked. It took every fiber of strength in his being to supplicate himself in this way, but he knew he could no longer simply barge in with impunity. Those days were over."

"What's this about?" Brett asked.

Their trance broken, several listeners turned around, glaring.

Dave mimed apology, then whispered, "That's Ron. He used to work in the mailroom, and everybody thought he was a dork because he'd memorized every Seinfeld episode. Now, people come to listen. And remember."

"Wow."

"Damn right, wow. That's talent. All those spreadsheets and PowerPoint decks I did? *This* is what brings people together. *This* is what lasts."

Eyes opened wide like Barrymore, Ron leaned in to face his rapt acolytes. "And then"—he paused expertly—"the great comedian asked him for his keys back."

The crowd gasped.

Not Raymond. "Ah, I've heard this one." They walked down another hallway to Raymond's office; Raymond turned to go in, then turned back.

"OMG, Bird and Squirrel are here."

"Y'know, Ron's not going to live forever. One day when he's gone, and I'm gone, and Dave and Martha—when all us old-timers are just so much dust, you'll get an office like mine. And you'll be the one to remember all this history and culture. So keep your ears open. And remember."

The office's intercom system crackled to life, and Martha's voice filled the air. "Ladies and gentlemen, please be prepared to 'Get into the Groove'…"

The door to the conference room closed. Raymond stood there at the entrance to his office, looking at nothing, preparing to receive. Brett heard him whisper, "God, I hope she can remember 'Disco Duck,' too."

—*Jeff Kulik*

THINGS THAT SURPRISED ME WHEN I MET GOD.

- The vocal fry
- Gets super-defensive when you mention Creation
- Really bad teeth
- Killed Jimi Hendrix to have someone to jam with
- Is on Twitter, but only has 36 followers
- Won't shut up about "Q"
- The buffet wasn't great
- "If you can beat Me in cornhole, I'll let you stay."
- Loves humans, but isn't *in love* with us
- Massive impostor syndrome
- I thought I saw a tentacle
- A soundtrack by Vangelis
- Whispered, "Kill me, *kill me*."
- Clearly hasn't read the Bible.

—*Damask Pugh*

HOW TO START A CONVERSATION WITH NEW PEOPLE.

Research has shown that having regular conversations with new people can increase a person's sense of well-being, enhance feelings of belonging, and reinforce social cohesion. What research doesn't tell us, however, is how one is supposed to go about this exactly. Most people, when faced with the prospect of speaking to someone for the first time, are immediately confronted by a number of common fears: What if they don't like me? What if I say something wrong? What will we talk about? Which way should I face? Which of their headparts should I look at while speaking?

"Well, a lot of us find it offensive."

Sadly, few know the answers to these questions. And fewer ever will.

Fortunately, Bystander Labs, being staffed entirely by cartoonists and comedy writers, is an authority on human sociality. To that end, we have compiled a list of proven techniques to help anyone overcome their confusion and become a skillful and magnetic conversationalist.

Who will I talk to?

Anyone. It's a free country. As long as you speak the same language and find yourselves in the same space, you are free to talk.

How should I dress?

Neatly, but not excessively formal. People tend to interpret the state of one's dress as an indicator of the state of their minds. Endeavor to look tidy, approachable, and pleasing.

Is there a better time of day to talk?

Yes: Nighttime. While people are so busy with their hectic modern lives during the day, at night they're generally at ease and open to new stimuli. Just walk right up and start conversing. You can do this during the day as well, of course. Just know that, like songbirds, humans are at their most calm when bathed in darkness.

How do I begin the conversation?

This is the number-one question we receive from people on this topic. In our research, we've found two approaches to be highly effective. The first is "question-asking." This works because people are always flattered when a stranger takes an interest in them. Asking questions tells them that you see them, and that you think they are interesting and unique. But what to ask? Some of our favorite starter questions are simple ones, including: "Who are you?" "In what city or village were you born?" and "What are your most cherished beliefs?" As your partner answers these questions, so too should you, matching disclosure with disclosure and establishing what is known as "rapport." "I am Charles," you might say. "I was born in Downeast Maine, and I believe that Hillary Clinton and Democratic elites are running a child sex-trafficking ring out of a Washington pizzeria." From there, the conversation should flow naturally.

But what if I am uncomfortable asking questions?

If you are uncomfortable asking questions, you can also utilize a second technique, called "triangulation." When you triangulate, you find something that you both are looking at, or experiencing, and simply remark upon it. You might say, "What a bird!" Or, "That was the loudest automobile I have heard in some time!" Or, "I can see that you are just as frightened as I am!" Acknowledging a shared experience will reassure your partner that you have something in common and serve as the basis for the conversation to come.

Which way should I face during my conversation?

North.

What do I do with my hands?

This is another very common question. Many have suggested keeping your hands at your sides, or behind your back, or in your pockets. But according to our research, there is only one appropriate place to put your hands: Hold them up in front of you, palms facing your partner, so he can see that you are not holding a dagger, and your hands are not smeared with blood or feces. This will tell your partner, "I am sane, and I mean you no harm." But also: "While I am putting myself at your mercy, know this, stranger: In the valley beyond there are a hundred killers who will spread your ribcage like the wings of a butterfly and feed you to the crows if you harm so much as a hair on my hand."

What parts of my partner's body should I focus most on?

The eyes, ears, and mouth are the most important parts of conversation, thus those are the only parts of your partner that you're allowed to touch —unless he becomes upset, at which time you may stroke his forehead with your tail.

What do I do if there is a lull in the conversation?

Whatever your partner said last, simply reply by asking, "Why?" You can also be more specific: "Why do you believe that happened?" or "Why have you stopped speaking all of a sudden?" This will rekindle the conversation.

What do I do if my partner becomes violent?

Since you will be holding your hands in front of you, simply draw a razor from your boot with your tail and put out the

DO YOU KNOW GINGER?
WE DO.

Created as the perfect conclusion to a great meal, Barrow's Intense is a cold pressed ginger liqueur, handcrafted in Brooklyn using more than 200lbs of fresh ginger per batch. Serve it over ice or add it to your favorite cocktail.

44 proof/22% ALC/VOL
Gluten Free, Vegan, Kosher Ⓚ

★★★★

4 Stars/Highly Recommended & Superb
F. Paul Pacult / Spirit Journal Sept 2014

A+
Good Spirits News

2014 CRAFT SPIRITS AWARDS GOLD

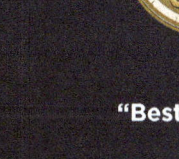
94
THE TASTING PANEL

"Best in Class"
SIP AWARDS 2013 PLATINUM

barrowsintense.com   @barrowsintense

light in his eyes.

What if I detect the possibility of friendship?

Studies show that seven out of ten random street encounters result in lasting friendship. If the conversation has gone so well that you think you might in time become friends, the next step is to exchange contact information. To do this, quickly plunge your tail into your partner's pocket and withdraw his phone. Once you have it, ask for his password, so you can enter your information in his contacts, along with a photo, and a detailed physical description of yourself. This description should cover not only appealing physical attributes, but also any that you might be deeply ashamed of.

When do I know the conversation is over?

The conversation is over when you say it is over.

—Joe Keohane

MY REVIEW OF MAD MEN: THE VIDEO GAME.

I was initially excited for Rockstar Games' newest offering. Not since *Sopranos: Flatbush Redemption* have we enjoyed a game based on a prestige television show. But while Rockstar's graphics were—as always—superb, I found the gameplay to be repetitive, limiting, and uninteresting.

The Story Mode begins when Don Draper wakes up on his office couch in a drunken haze, upon which one is instructed to "Press A to ASK THE SECRETARY FOR COFFEE." The gameplay continues when Don delivers a pitch at the Dow Chemical meeting, where one basically has two choices: improvising a spiel, or using the previously written copy. After choosing "Improvise," I must admit that I was entertained to see Don win over the client with a long and rousing speech touching on a real news item from 1962. But upon finishing the meeting, there were only two options: "Press A to HAVE DRINKS WITH ROGER," or "Press B to LOCK YOURSELF IN YOUR OFFICE."

Free Play Mode is similarly uninspiring. Don has full range of Sterling Cooper, but is able to do little more than enter his coworkers' offices and engage them in conversation. I was pleased to see that this mode also enables one to play as Peggy, although this quickly gets old, as unlike Don, she only has access to her secretary's desk and the women's bathroom.

Fans of *Mad Men* might enjoy the game's dialogue, but both its Story and Free Play Modes are utterly forgettable. TWO STARS.

—Jake Houston

Follow Peter Kuper,

Reuben and Eisner award-winning author,

into the heart of an immense darkness

In stores 11.5.2019

"Not only a triumph of graphic art but a compelling work of literary interpretation. [Kuper] has designed a masterful synthesis that retains Conrad's language while pressing beyond the limits of Conrad's vision."

—Maya Jasanoff, Coolidge Professor of History, Harvard University, from the foreword

Learn more at peterkuper.com

W. W. Norton & Company
wwnorton.com | @wwnorton

"As a deeply uncomfortable depressed Midwest person, I relate to this excruciatingly hilarious book more than I'd like to admit."

—SAMANTHA IRBY,
New York Times best-selling author

"Hilarious, warm, relatable, confessional, and emotional. Her writing leaps off the page! But not literally. That would be horrible. Imagine writing leaping off the page, soiling your house. Just awful."

— MEGAN AMRAM,
writer/producer of
The Good Place & The Simpsons

ESSAYS on the AWKWARD, UNCOMFORTABLE, SURPRISINGLY REGULAR PARTS of BEING HUMAN

including

My Dog Explains My Weekly Schedule • Depression Isn't a Competition, but, Like, Why Aren't I Winning? • Mustache Lady • White Friend Confessional • Treating Objects Like Women

HarperOne   An Imprint of HarperCollins Publishers   www.harperone.com

OLD SCHOLL

BY MICHAEL PERSHAN

SUBJECT: RE: SOME VERY SERIOUS ISSUES

To: velonica@happyrainbow.com
From: michael@verycheapsyringes.com

Velonica,
Your email of the 23rd was shocking. Normally, I would not privilege such drivel with a response, but it was full of so many objectionable statements that I feel I must speak.

As you know, things lately have been absolutely awful for our family. As I explained, Josephine's brother was mauled to death under mysterious circumstances, and so there's been a lot of stress. One would hope that kindergarten would be a respite, a safe haven, but no—Josephine has been miserable at Happy Rainbow.

All we have heard is complaint after complaint from Josephine's teachers. Come on! It's her first year in school. I'm not saying it hasn't been a rocky start. But do you want to know how many times Josephine bit another child before she entered your school? Zero. And yet you're so sure that she is biting other children now. Doesn't that seem just a little suspicious?

Yes, her teeth are "incredibly sharp, like a steel trap lined with razorblades." Thank you for noticing.

You've told us that the bitings happened on Josephine's first day of school, also on her second day of school, days three through nineteen and every other day since, and that the other children are terrified. Well, we are terrified as well. We are terrified at what they may be doing to Josephine's self-image.

Josephine is (obviously) quite large. Smaller children (i.e. all children) naturally ostracize her. I would expect that as the principal, you'd try to make things better. But instead—keeping her "a minimum of twenty feet from the other students?" My God. What do you do when a kid eats paste? Shoot them and use their skin as a rug?

And, yes, Josephine is very hairy. I am even OK with calling her "furry." We believe this is a glandular condition. But you, a non-doctor, are "quite sure" she is not human and is clearly a "bear dressed in children's clothing." Quite sure? Well! Shots fired.

You say "Josephine will only eat raw salmon" like we don't know this. Some kids won't eat anything but pizza or hot dogs—what about "We will accommodate any dietary issues?" Was that just sell copy for the website?

Potty training: Once again, kids learn at different rates. I can't believe I have to tell you that. We say again, the diapers would stay on if your staff would simply use the correct amount of tape.

And it is perfectly normal for Josephine to struggle when you try to apply the correct amount of tape. By the way, how is Mrs. Tonya doing? Can you check to see if she got the flowers we sent? Josephine clearly mistook her for a salmon. It happens.

Finally, you suggest finding a school "better suited for Josephine's needs because she is not a human but a bear and she belongs in a zoo." It's like, what are you even saying? What does this even mean?

Velonica, if you have something to say, just come out and say it. But wearing pink is simply a bad idea. Especially near snack time.

Best Wishes,
Michael

MICHAEL PERSHAN *is a writer and math teacher in NYC. "And that's pretty much as far as I can go without triggering waves of self-doubt," he says.*

FACTS

BY STEVE YOUNG
BACK IN THE DAY
The American Century was weirder than you remember

AUTHORITIES CONDUCTED nightly checks to ensure women displayed no Communist tendencies such as armpit hair.

SHOPLIFTERS SHOWED merchants what they were taking, so merchants could keep accurate records of how much money they were losing.

RADIO PURCHASERS had to sign affidavits affirming that they would observe proper radio-listening dress codes.

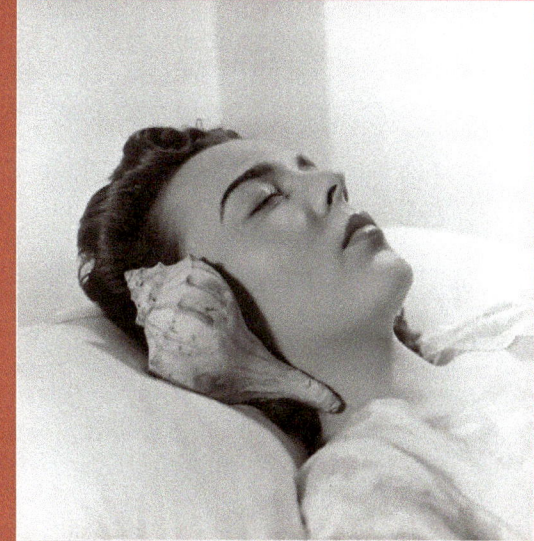

THOUGH THE 1954 FILM *The Creature From the Black Lagoon* was a hit, audiences responded poorly to the sequel, *Rampaging Mollusks*.

IN THE YEARS AFTER WWII, "I personally poked Hitler!" was an effective pickup line.

THE YEAR 1949 saw the first crude prototype of Matt Damon.

STEVE YOUNG

(@pantssteve) is a veteran Letterman *writer who's also written for* The Simpsons. *He's the main subject of the award-winning documentary,* Bathtubs Over Broadway.

#CHANGES
BY LARRY DOYLE
WE ARE MAKING CHANGES
It's a time to come together and make things better. For us.

In these troubled times, we are making Changes, and not just to this voiceover, which we've recast from Raspy Cowboy to *Working Woman IV*, soothing without being motherly or otherwise gendered. We are also replacing this font, which our Graphic Diversity Group has determined to be problematically Germanic.

And rest assured we will be making additional Changes, so many and very, very soon.

Because we get it. We get *you*. Our bots have been scrubbing your social media and deleted social media for Actionable Gestures, and our drones have been swooping down on your Grievance Events, scanning your clever and important signs, and your faces.

This data, along with our proprietary Advanced Grokking Software, will allow us to be able to give you more than lip service to any of the following.

We understand your loss. It's what, a couple of thousand bucks? Meanwhile we've lost literally billions of dollars—admittedly billions we didn't have last December—but think about how you'd feel if you had temporarily lost even *one* billion dollars. That's more money than you will ever see in your lifetime, and likely can even comprehend. Yet, Jerome Powell coughs,* and *POOF*, that's a few billion we might not make up this quarter.

So, yes, we know what it's like to worry about not being able to buy eggs or whatever, as well as staying up at night thinking about the scary financial challenges ahead, such as losing your home, etc. Recently we were forced to sell one of our islands due to short-term illiquidity, and also because it was sinking. Further impacting us, our kids' school is going fully airborne this fall, with a fleet of converted Airbus A380s refueling in air and flying twenty-four hours a day, and Headmaster says he can't even begin to estimate what that might cost. We know what it's like to have economic uncertainty, too.

We feel your pain, somewhat vaguely, but we're working towards acuity. We did a past-life regression, but the worst we could come up with was Lord Mountbatten, who had to live in India before air conditioning and who, after all, was blown up in the end.

---
* You needn't concern yourself with who this is.

We also received experimental empathy therapy, similar to the Ludovico technique used in *A Clockwork Orange*, only we were allowed to close our eyes if we wanted to, and instead of sexual brutality we were forced to watch your most popular Tik-Toks, and rather than Beethoven it was scored to Supertramp.

We fear your fears. We, too, are terrified of this plague you've been spreading and are spending untold sums to develop small-batch vaccines. If it makes sense, we are confident we can scale this cure and offer it to you at an allowable mark-up. (We are already furnishing masks free-of-charge to those of you who can't be rousted from in front of our buildings).

We feel unsafe, just like you. Consequently, we have been buying up gun manufacturers and chemical plants to better secure our perimeter, but also to ensure you have the tools you need to protect yourselves from the police.

We want to be more *like* you. Not specifically, but proportionately. In order to plump our Diversity Numbers, we have been working night and day coming up with whole new types of minorities. So, in addition to our court-ordered Affirmative Interviewing Program, run by Maria Woo-Laughing Feather (an Asian-Indigenous Latina, who is also L or B or Q, we are pretty sure), we will be reaching out to some truly underrepresented populations: your Welsh-Canadians, Luxembourgers, cyborgs at least 65% human, and certain whales. We'll let you know how we're doing at our next annual meeting—where we fully expect you to keep our feet to the fire, though you'll need to be a stockholder to do that.

Of course no real Change can be accomplished without **changing what is inside us**.

And that starts with us acknowledging all of the advantages we've received through our Privilege and Entitlement.

There, we said it.

As we amass and test and perhaps someday implement these forward-facing mods, we ask for your patience and continued patronage. Don't thank us; **thank *you***. B

LARRY DOYLE (@thelarrydoyle) *is a frequent contributor to* **The New Yorker**. *His first novel,* I Love You, Beth Cooper, *won the 2008 Thurber Prize for American Humor and was made into a movie.*

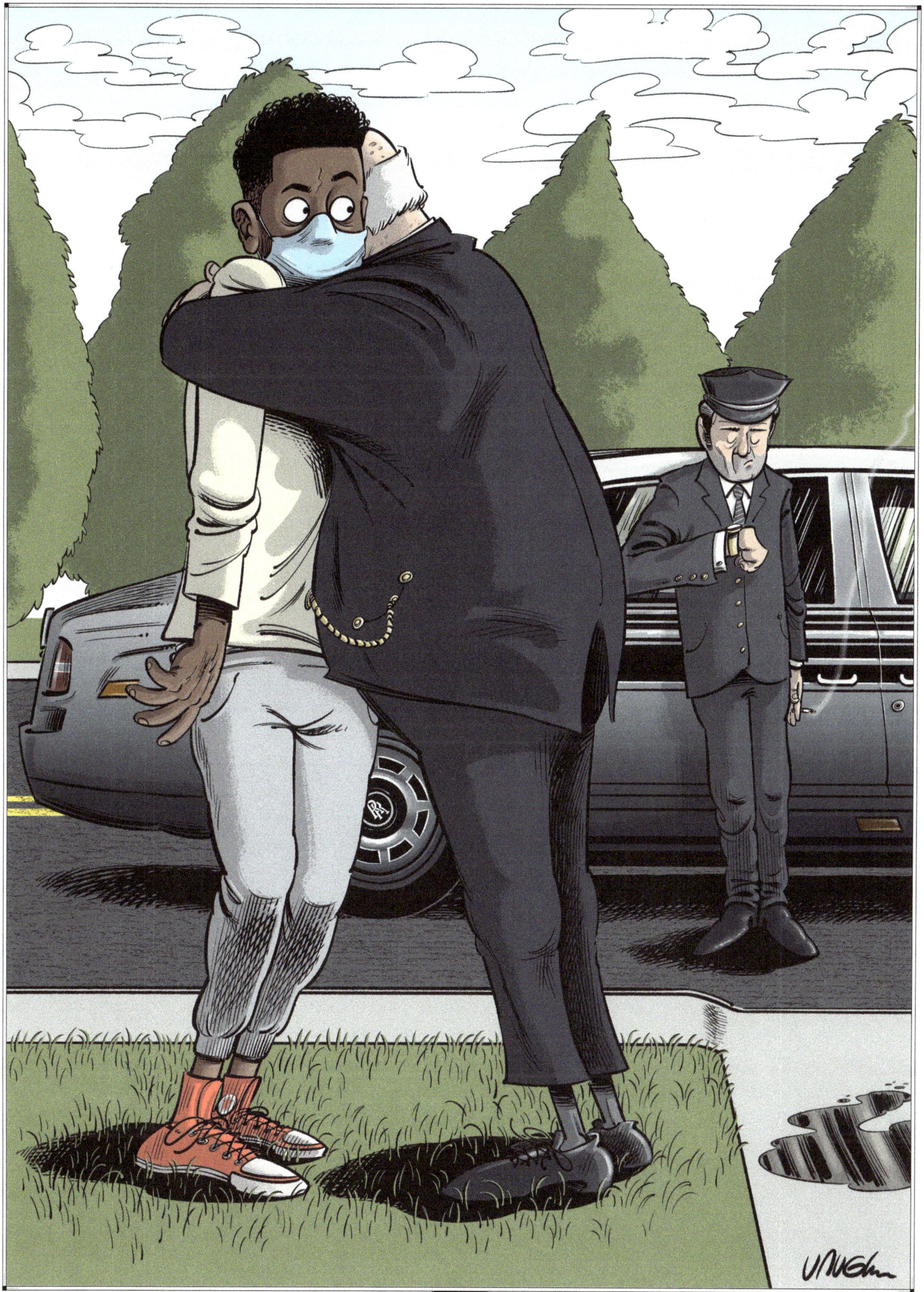

SILVER LININGS
BY BOB ECKSTEIN

I HAVE NOW PERFECTED MY SIGNATURE DISH: LEMON PASTA

Zest 3 large lemons. Squeeze their juice in a bowl with a ⅓ cup of Extra Virgin olive oil. Add fresh ground pepper, whisk and put aside with CNN on in the background.

Carmelize in a pan 12 oz. package (4 links) chicken apple saugage sliced into wheels. Use grease as well.

Boil 1 lb. of ziti pasta till al dente (I use Cara Mamma's artisan Paccheri when on sale or if I sell something on Craig's List).

Halve two containers of grape tomatoes, track down a cup of shaved Parmesan cheese and pick all the leaves off a small basil plant.

Mix all ingredients in a large bowl. Serves 6.

BOB ECKSTEIN is a New York Times *bestselling illustrator and the world's leading snowman expert* (The Illustrated History of the Snowman). *He teaches writing and drawing at NYU.*

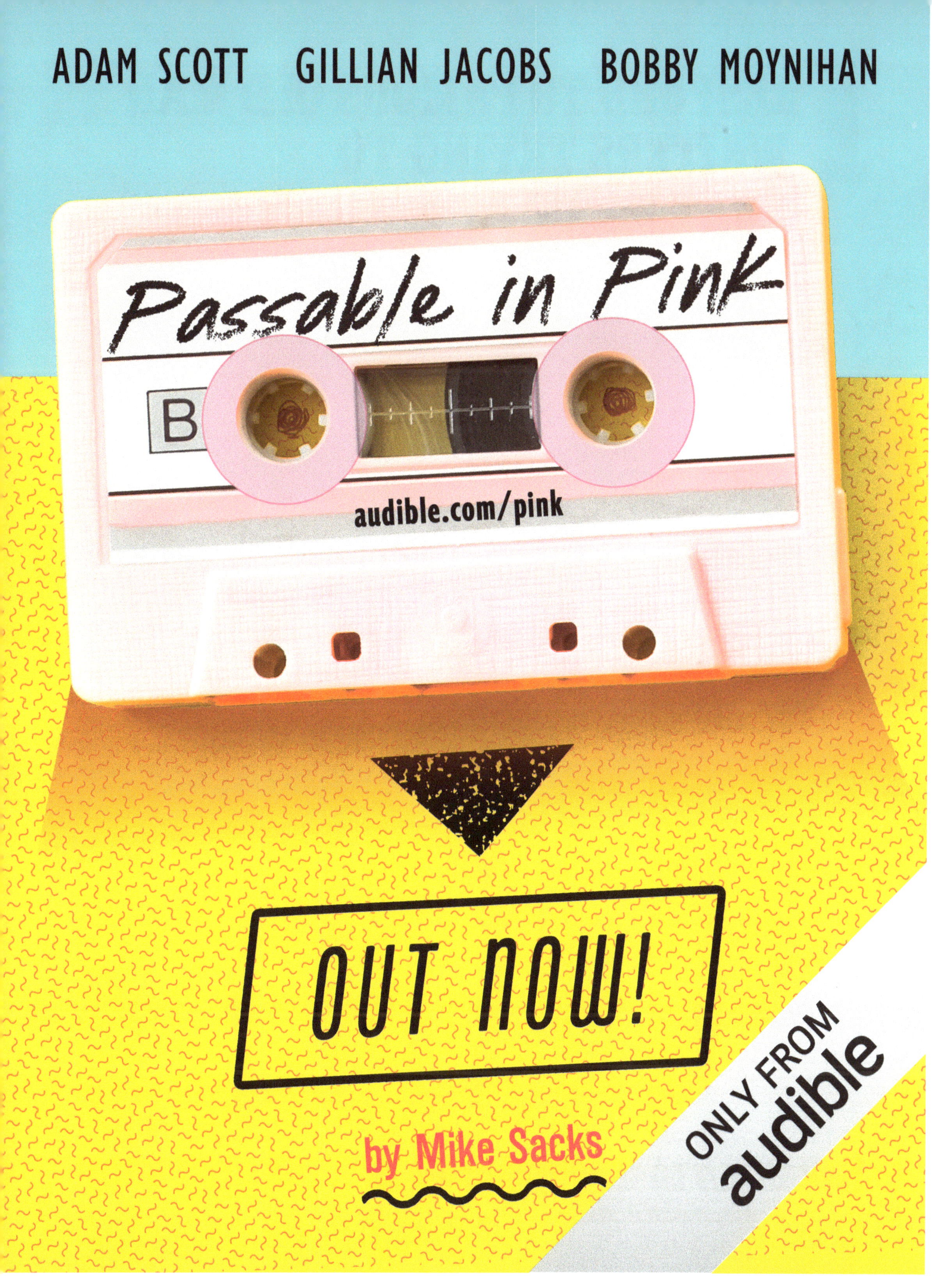
ADAM SCOTT
GILLIAN JACOBS
BOBBY MOYNIHAN
Passable in Pink
B
audible.com/pink
OUT NOW!
by Mike Sacks
ONLY FROM
audible

ANTAGONISTS
BY SARAH HUTTO

I RESPOND TO FAMOUS OLD MAN WRITERS TRYING TO CHAT ME UP AT A PARTY

George Orwell: All animals are equal, but some animals are more equal than others.
Me: So I guess you're not like, a total vegan then.

James Joyce: Mistakes are the portals of discovery.
Me: Oh, thanks for the heads-up—I was wondering what kind of brownies those were.

Herman Melville: Better to sleep with a sober cannibal than a drunken Christian.
Me: Have you thought of trying a dating site that's not specifically geared toward farmers?

Cormac McCarthy: Keep a little fire burning. However small. However hidden.
Me: Actually, Steve said you can just smoke on the porch.

Ernest Hemingway: There is nothing to writing. All you do is sit down at a typewriter and bleed.
Me: I've been bleeding for six days. Do you have your typewriter with you?

Charles Dickens: No one is useless in this world who lightens the burdens of another.
Me: Okay, do you still need me to hold this laptop bag, though?

John Updike: Being naked approaches being revolutionary; going barefoot is mere populism.
Me: Still, you should probably zip up.

Vladimir Nabokov: I think like a genius, I write like a distinguished author, and I speak like a child.
Me: Wow, you're right. That is the most disturbing Elmo impression I've ever heard.

Walt Whitman: I am large—I contain multitudes.
Me: Wow, I don't even think multitudes count toward my deductible.

Edgar Allen Poe: The death of a beautiful woman is, unquestionably, the most poetical topic in the world.
Me: Did something happen to Beyoncé?

Truman Capote: I believe more in the scissors than I do in the pencil.
Me: I believe in the Twitter "Drafts" folder.

T.S. Eliot: Do I dare disturb the universe?
Me: Someone's in here!

Franz Kafka: Don't bend; don't water it down; don't try to make it logical; don't edit your own soul according to the fashion. Rather, follow your most intense obsessions mercilessly.
Me: So, you don't think I should return the pants?

F. Scott Fitzgerald: The test of a first-rate intelligence is the ability to hold two opposed ideas in the mind at the same time, and still retain the ability to function.
Me: No, you have to pick—Beatles or Stones?

William Faulkner: There is something about jumping a horse over a fence, something that makes you feel good. Perhaps it's the risk, the gamble. In any event it's a thing I need.
Me: I'm like that, but with picking up bodega cats.

John Cheever: I can't write without a reader. It's precisely like a kiss—you can't do it alone.
Me: You'd be surprised what you can order online nowadays.

Norman Mailer: Writing books is the closest men ever come to childbearing.
Me: You've written a lot of books. Your pelvic floor must be a mess.

Mark Twain: Rumors of my death have been greatly exaggerated.
Me: I mean, not really.

SARAH HUTTO (@huttopian) *is a contributor to* The New Yorker, The New York Times, *and* McSweeney's. *She is currently working on finishing a novel she started reading two years ago.*

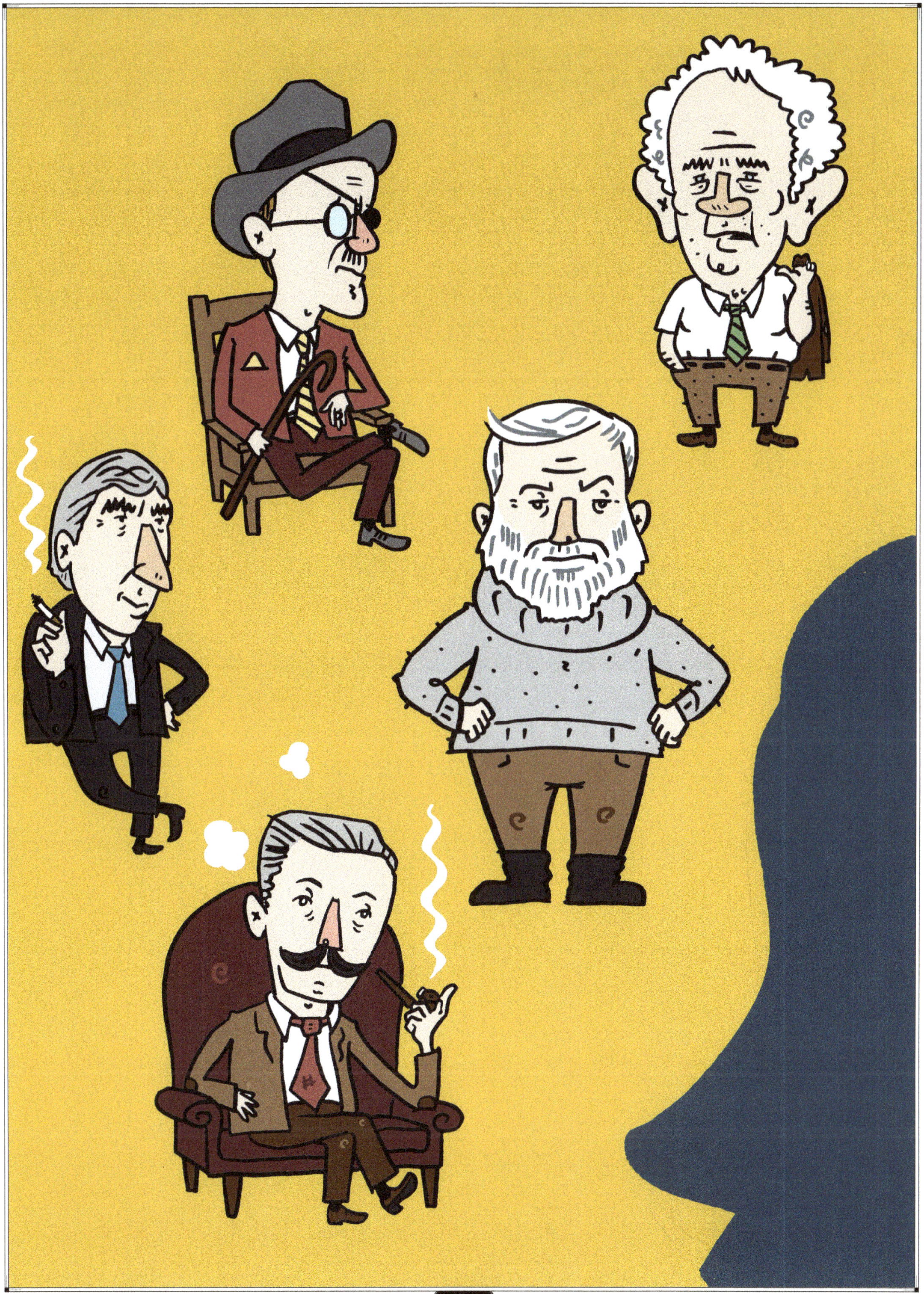

LANCE HANSEN

SELF! HELP!

BY LARS KENSETH

GIVE YOURSELF A PAT ON THE MIND!

Chances are, you've heard of Psychology. Maybe you've seen the word used in self-help books, or in the glossy pages of *Extraordinary Rendition* magazine. It's a field of unparalleled depth and breadth, which is why it's often called "The Mall of America of sciences." But did you know Psychology can help you lose weight?

I've struggled with weight my whole life, and thought it was because I was *no darn good*. But now I know that it's not my fault—it's just that my brain is one big Gordian knot of bad habits and adverse associations. No diet, cleanse or exercise belt would make a lick of difference until I fixed what's up *here*. I'm tapping on my head now.

Psychology says, the easiest way to lose weight is by substituting healthy options for your unhealthy cravings. I know it sounds counterintuitive, but if you're clever enough about mimicking your favorite foods with wholesome ingredients, you will *trick your mind* into forming healthier habits. Don't believe me? Check out these examples:

- Tummy rumbling for chicken wings? Try some tasty "cauliflower wings" instead. Delicious, right?
- Instead of pizza, treat yourself to some portobello mushroom caps with tomatoes and a light dusting of low-flavor, part-skim Mozzarella. Mm-MMMM—my mouth is watering already.
- Hankering for a double cheeseburger? Satisfy that urge by stacking rice cake "patties" on rice cake "buns." Where do I back up the yum truck?

"But Lars," you say, "these seem like pretty lazy facsimiles. I'm paying ten dollars a month for this weight-loss app you basically forced on me. I expect better." A challenge? I accept! Here are some recipes that are sure to light up your taste buds—and *your mind buds*.

- Everybody loves cheesecake. But know what's just as satisfying? Chia seeds poured into a springform pan with a quart of non-fat Greek yogurt. Boom goes the flavor-mite!
- Eyyyy, who wants-a da pizza? More like, eyyy, who wants-a da rice flour lavash smothered in cilantro, agar agar and one cherry tomato. That's-a spicy health ball!
- Wondering whether you'll be able to make it another day without French fries? Why not jam an unripe avocado in your eye?

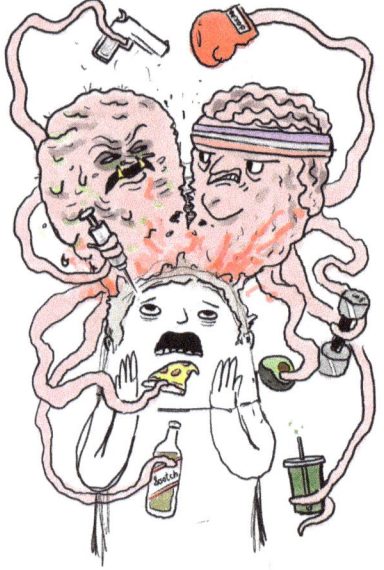

"Lars, jamming an avocado in your eye is not a recipe," you whine. And you're right, whiner—but it is Psychology.

It's called "negative reinforcement," but you can think of it as Psychology's "bad cop." Whenever you've got a hostile witness (French fries), sometimes it's best to put out a cigarette on his tongue (eye-avocado) and find out what he knows. *We're not messing around here, asshole!* (that was me talking to your unhealthy habits) I'm sorry, what did you say? You want your lawyer? I can't understand you because I just burned your tongue! (figuratively)

I see you're walking out of the room and now I'm just talking to myself. This is what psychologists call "giving up"—one of the many challenges you'll encounter while trying to lose weight. Friends will peer pressure you, co-workers will badger you and loved ones will intervene, concerned for your mental health. Obviously, the smart thing to do is to cut them out of your life and change your name. But for a lot of people that's just not an option. If that's you, avail yourself of one of these hot tips:

- Going to the movies? Skip the large butter popcorn with the hot dog crown. Instead, bring a head of broccoli from home in a lunchpail full of wheat germ. All hail the new King Popcorn!
- Does a buddy want to meet up for happy hour appetizers? Instead, convince them to put on some eye black and sprint through a state forest. Afterwards, reward yourselves with some plump, juicy pine cones. Can I get an *mmm-mmm*?
- Feel like drowning your sorrows in bourbon after alienating everyone you love? Consider an alternative: running into the night with no phone or wallet until your legs give out, forcing you to crawl to the nearest gas station for help. [*chef's kiss*]

Remember, the key to re-shaping your body is re-shaping your mind. If you're anything like me, after a couple weeks that seem like years, you'll wake up in a cabin that isn't yours with the lock jimmied and tire tracks that stop in the dirt driveway — but with no signs of a car—and realize that you did it! Give yourself a pat on the back—or should I say, a pat on the mind?

LARS KENSETH (@larskenseth) *is a cartoonist for* **The New Yorker**, *a Sundance Fellow and is currently baking a big loaf of weird for* **Adult Swim**. *Feel free to troll him on Instagram.*

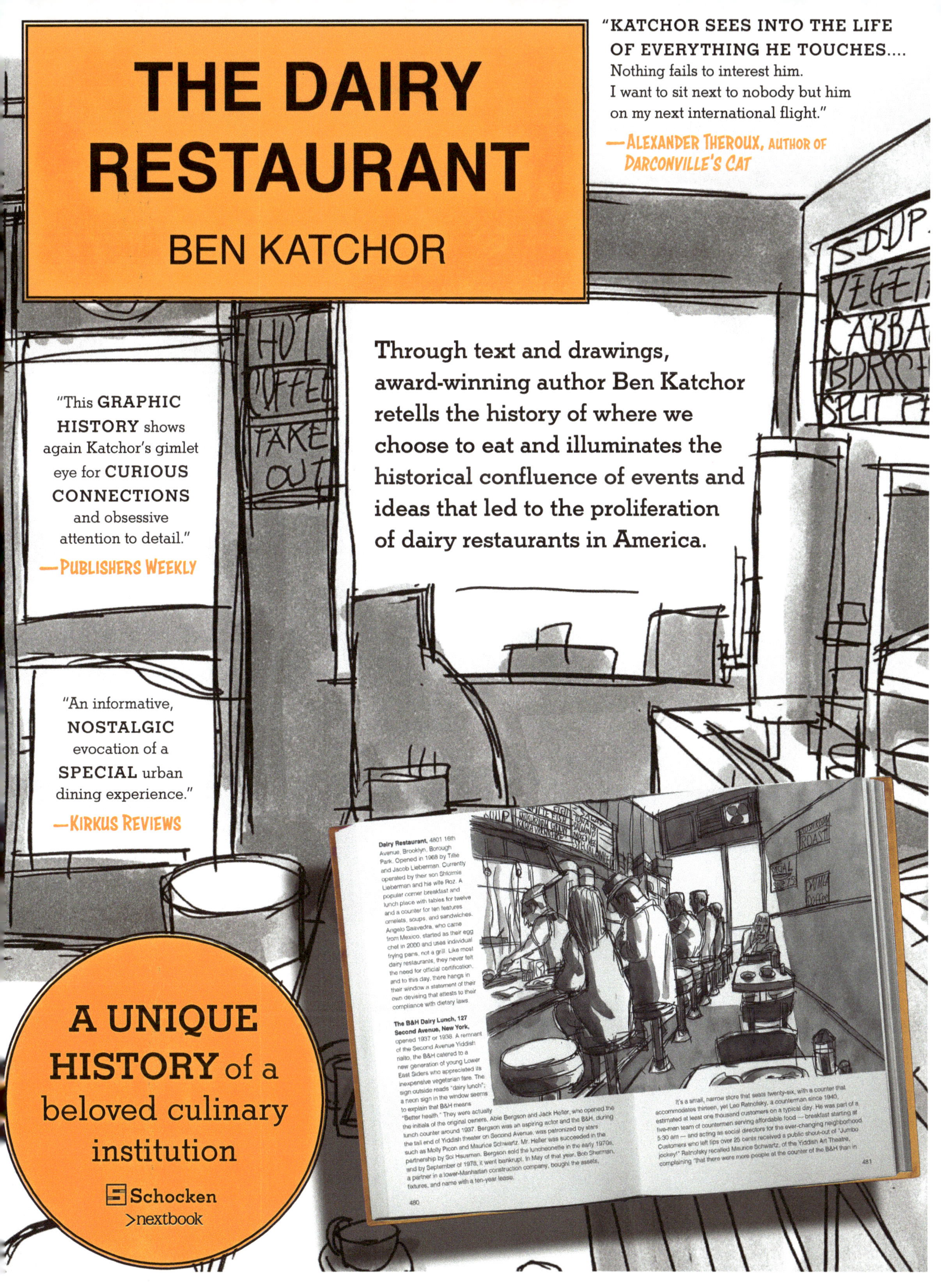
THE DAIRY RESTAURANT
BEN KATCHOR
"KATCHOR SEES INTO THE LIFE OF EVERYTHING HE TOUCHES.... Nothing fails to interest him. I want to sit next to nobody but him on my next international flight."
—ALEXANDER THEROUX, AUTHOR OF DARCONVILLE'S CAT
HOT COFFEE TAKE OUT
SOUP VEGET CABBA BORSCH SPLIT PE
Through text and drawings, award-winning author Ben Katchor retells the history of where we choose to eat and illuminates the historical confluence of events and ideas that led to the proliferation of dairy restaurants in America.
"This GRAPHIC HISTORY shows again Katchor's gimlet eye for CURIOUS CONNECTIONS and obsessive attention to detail."
—PUBLISHERS WEEKLY
"An informative, NOSTALGIC evocation of a SPECIAL urban dining experience."
—KIRKUS REVIEWS
Dairy Restaurant, 4801 16th Avenue, Brooklyn, Borough Park. Opened in 1968 by Tillie and Jacob Lieberman. Currently operated by their son Shloimie Lieberman and his wife Roz. A popular corner breakfast and lunch place with tables for twelve and a counter for ten features omelets, soups, and sandwiches. Angelo Saavedra, who came from Mexico, started as their egg chef in 2000 and uses individual frying pans, not a grill. Like most dairy restaurants, they never felt the need for official certification, and to this day, there hangs in their window a statement of their own devising that attests to their compliance with dietary laws.
The B&H Dairy Lunch, 127 Second Avenue, New York, opened 1937 or 1938. A remnant of the Second Avenue Yiddish rialto, the B&H catered to a new generation of young Lower East Siders who appreciated its inexpensive vegetarian fare. The sign outside reads "dairy lunch"; a neon sign in the window seems to explain that B&H means "Better health." They were actually the initials of the original owners, Abie Bergson and Jack Heller, who opened the lunch counter around 1937. Bergson was an aspiring actor and the B&H, during the tail end of Yiddish theater on Second Avenue, was patronized by stars such as Molly Picon and Maurice Schwartz. Mr. Heller was succeeded in the partnership by Sol Hausman. Bergson sold the luncheonette in the early 1970s, and by September of 1978, it went bankrupt. In May of that year, Bob Sherman, a partner in a lower-Manhattan construction company, bought the assets, fixtures, and name with a ten-year lease.
480
SOUP
ROAST
It's a small, narrow store that seats twenty-six, with a counter that accommodates thirteen, yet Leo Ratnofsky, a counterman since 1940, estimated at least one thousand customers on a typical day. He was part of a five-man team of countermen serving affordable food — breakfast starting at 5:30 am — and acting as social directors for the ever-changing neighborhood. Customers who left tips over 25 cents received a public shout-out of "Jumbo jockey!" Ratnofsky recalled Maurice Schwartz, of the Yiddish Art Theatre, complaining "that there were more people at the counter of the B&H than in
481
A UNIQUE HISTORY of a beloved culinary institution
Schocken
>nextbook

Potty training can be a PRICKLY issue.

Laugh out loud with this picture book about a family *attempting* to potty train their new pet porcupine, from *New Yorker* cartoonist Tom Toro. You may almost wet your pants giggling.

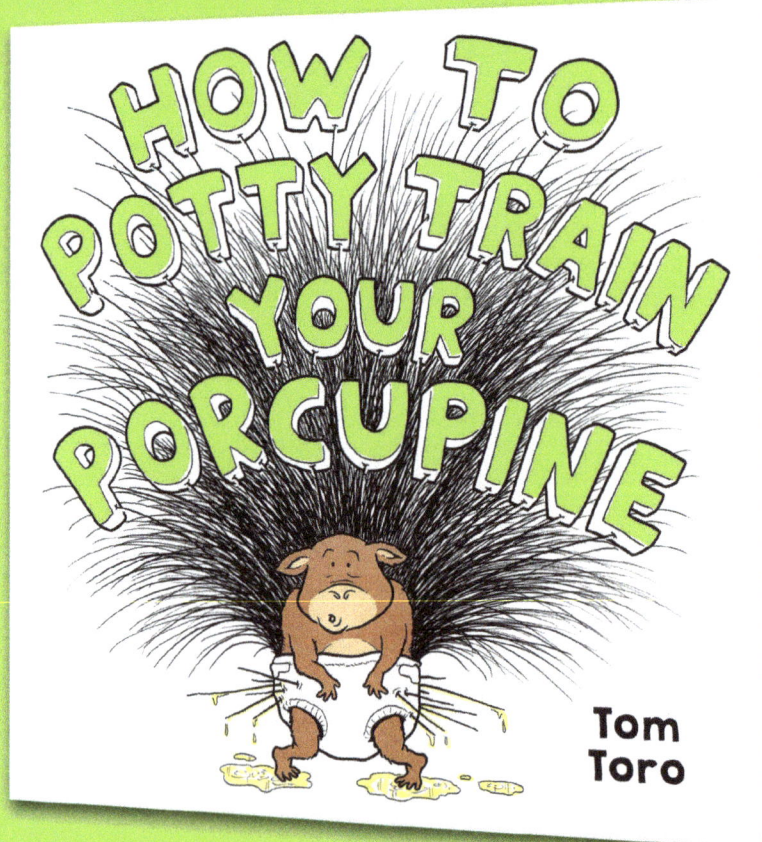

HOW TO POTTY TRAIN YOUR PORCUPINE

Tom Toro

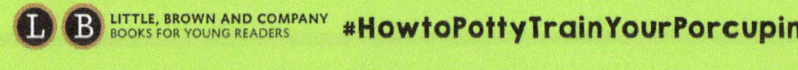

LITTLE, BROWN AND COMPANY
BOOKS FOR YOUNG READERS

#HowtoPottyTrainYourPorcupine I LBYR.com

WELCOME to WOODMONT College

NO REFUNDS!

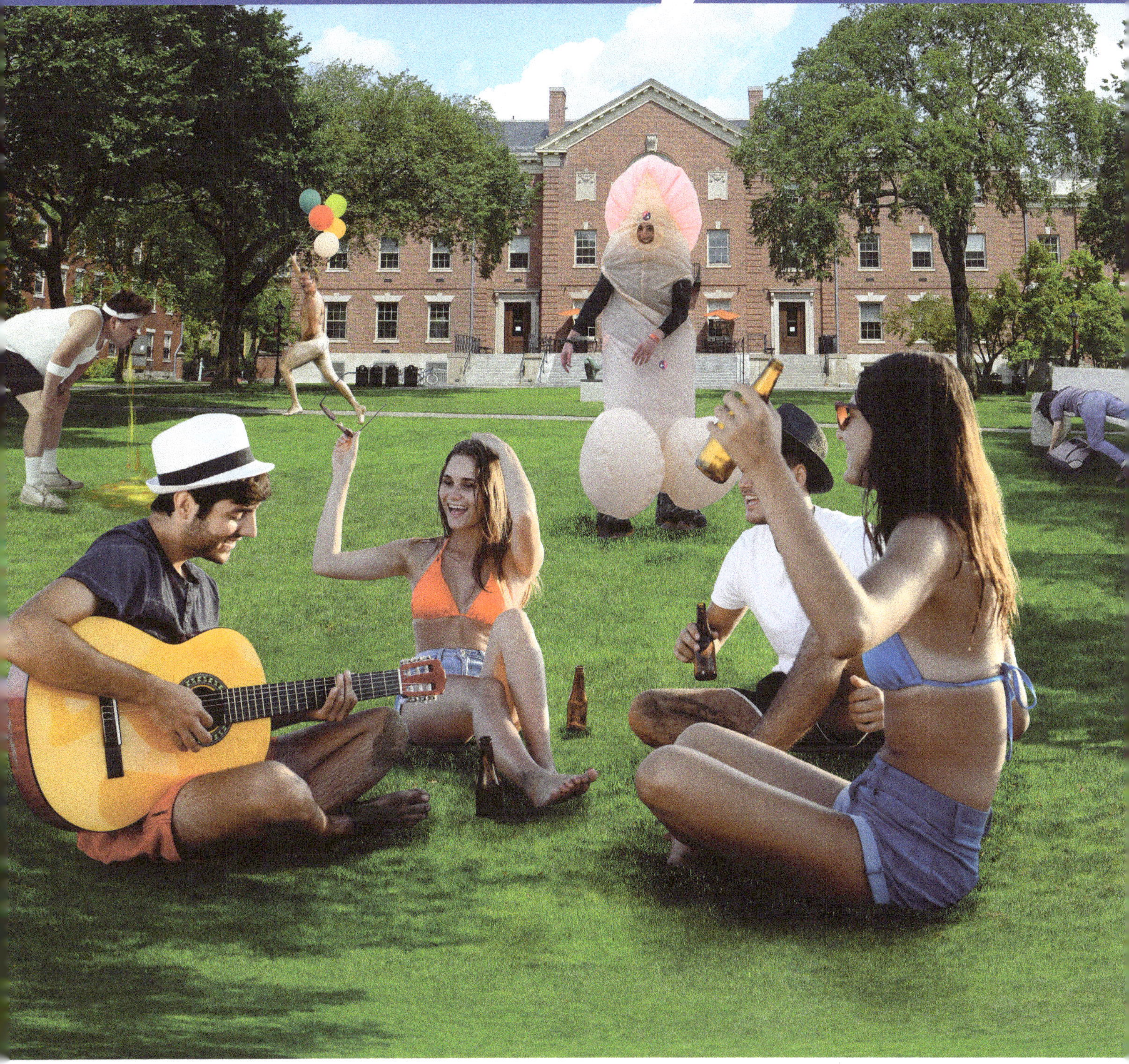

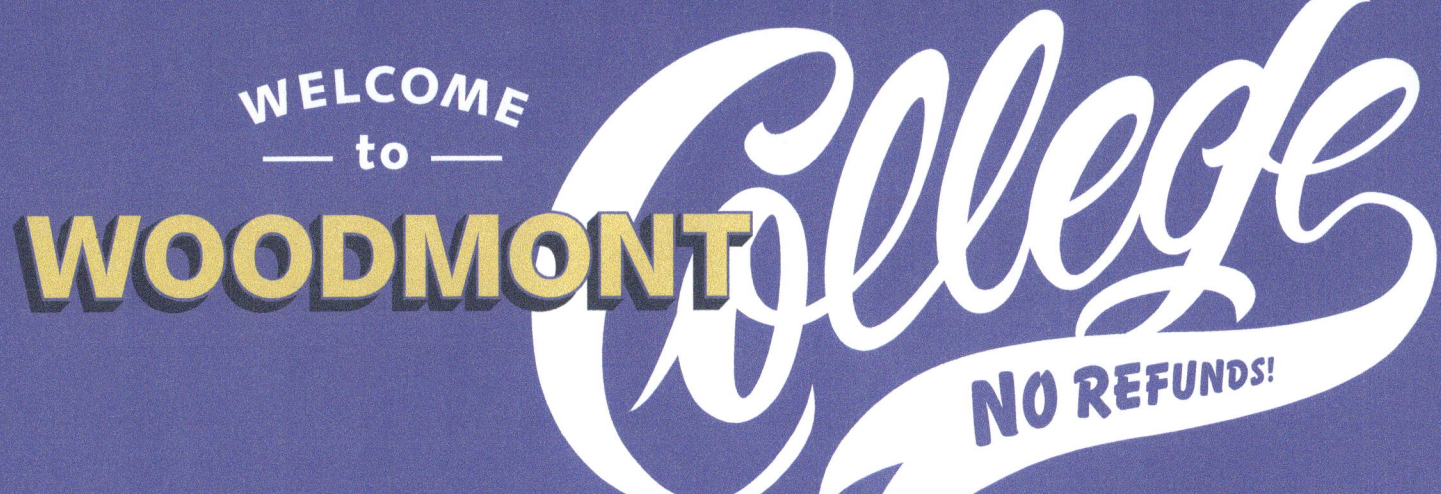

"Knowledge is priceless; never more so than when you pay for it."

TABLE OF CONTENTS | 3

Welcome From Four Disgraced Chancellors And Our Current Chancellor 6

An Institution Redefining "Accredited" 8
    Our Mission Statement 9
    Our Motto: "To Let Fear of Knowledge
        Be Dragged Out to Sea" 10
    Our Fight Song, Starship's "Nothing's Gonna
        Stop Us Now," and the Reason We Spent
        40 Percent of Our Endowment to Secure
        the Rights to It 11
    Woodmont College: A Highly Selective
        Timeline 13

About Today's Woodmont 16
    Woodmont at a Glance Through Stats in
        Catchy, Colorful Font and Stunning Widely-
        Available Infographic Templates 18
    We Welcome Our Transfer Students
        from Trump University! 21
    There's More to Life Than Just Test Scores!
        Why High School Guidance Counselors
        Can't Always Be Trusted 24
    Why *Playboy* Party School Rankings
        Can Always Be Trusted 28
    Retention and Graduation Rates: Four Year,
        Six Year ... and Career Fifty-Year-
        Old Students You Will Notice Drinking
        Coffee and Talking to Themselves in
        Der Rat Skeller 30
    Freshman Class Size: Are Binoculars Needed? ... 33
    Meet Sparky, Our Dean of Admissions.
        He's Quite a Character! And Yes,
        That's a Raccoon on His Shoulder.
        And Yes, It's Dead. 37

The Importance Of Diversity At Woodmont College As Of June 2019 By Court Order 39

The *US News* College Ranking System And What It Gets So Wrong About Woodmont College 44
    Is Your Donation to Our Legal Team in *Woodmont vs. US News* Now Tax Deductible? 49

Accredited in all the *Right* Places. C'mon. Let Us Show You Where. 51
    Why We're No Longer Woodmont *University* 53

The Coronavirus Nightmare of 2020 56
    An explanation about our 87% Coronavirus positive rate 58
    You Can Sue All You Want: Our NO REFUND Policy 61
    If You Still Have a Child Stuck Overseas on Semester Abroad 63
    Why This Will Never Happen Again: Our Brand-New Public Quarantine 64
    Shame Tank for Coronavirus-Positive Students Designed by the Architect Responsible for New York City's 9/11 Memorial............ 69

You Might Have Seen Our Ads in the Back of High Times? 71
    Do you recall the specific discount code for your 15% off? 75

A Dump Truck and More: The Woodmont College Seal 77
    Why the Eagle Is Holding a Bloody, Severed Chicken Head......................... 79
    Why the Seal's Text is Written in Comic Sans and Balloon Font 83
    Why "Higher" in "Higher Education" is Spelled Incorrectly............................ 85

The Asterisk Next to Our Lone Nobel Prize ... 87

The Importance of Diversity at Woodmont College, As of June 2016 by Court Order 89

A Different Kind Of Qualified: Our Position On Legacy Students............... 90
    We Don't Like Them Anymore Than You Do 92
    The Only Half-True "Erik and Kyle Mendendez Were Accepted Into Woodmont" Rumors............................ 95

Alcohol And Controlled Substances 98
    Our Zero Tolerance Policy on Bath Salts 103
    The Woodmont Drinking-Olympics Doping Scandal of 2018 105
    Meet Roger, Our Ninety-Six-Year Old Jitney Driver for Tipsy Students 109
    If You *Must*, Buckets Are On Us: Ayahuasca Experimentation 114

Learning at Woodmont.......................... 116
    Understanding the Neural Implant Received at Registration 117
    Understanding Your Chinese, Russian or Israeli Adjunct 119
    Academic Calendar............................... 123
    Academic Calendar with the Understanding That Wednesday Nights Are the *True* Start of the Weekend........ 127

Our Curriculum (Excluding Quantam Physics, Due To an Atom-Smashing and Particle Collider Gone Haywire At the Spring '11 Departmental Picnic)................ 134

You Have To At Least Try: Academic Requirements 137
    Majoring in Social Media Influencing: It's Not Just for Idiots Anymore............... 139
    Weighted GPAs: Why 3.0 is the New 1.0 and Vice-Versa 145

High School Extracurricular Activities:
   Why Spanish Club Just Ain't Gonna
   Cut It. *Comprende?* 149
Samples of Successful Application Essays........ 151
Samples of Unsuccessful Application Essays 156
Samples of Application Essays We Immediately
   Shredded and Fed to the Hogs 167

**Academic Requirements For Students
Whose Parents Have Campus Facilities
Named After Them** 174

**God Forbid Education Should
Inconvenience You In The Slightest:
Online Studies** 178
   No, Don't Even Get Dressed. Let *Us* Do
      All the Work. We're Being Sarcastic.......... 183

**Learning While A Sicilian Fisherman
Palpates Your Breasts: Studying Abroad** 187

**It's Never Too Late in Life to Find
Yourself in Tremendous Debt** 190
   Non-Traditional Students 194
   Incredibly "Non-Traditional" Students:
      You Just Won't Believe What
      You're Seeing 199

**Teacher/Student Relationships:
What's Allowed, What's Not,
What's Mandatory** 201
   Penalties for Plagiarism, Academic
      Dishonesty, and Too Much
      Academic Integrity........................... 204
   Avoiding the Skeezy Dude Who Writes
      Term Papers for the Free Booze in the
      Back Booth of the Local Watering Hole..... 207

**Real-World Humiliation Your
Parents Paid For: Woodmont Sponsored
Internships**.. 215

The Agony Of Freedom: Graduation 222
   Late fee assessed for diplomas held more
      than three hours.............................. 226
   Digital or Hard Copy or Us Just Telling
      You "You're Now a Graduate"?............... 229
   No Tie-Dyed Shirt, No Flip-Flops, No Funny
      Saying on Mortar Board, No Diploma! 231

**Who You'll Be Parroting For A Year
Or Two: Faculty**.................................... 234
   What Our Faculty's Facial Tattoos Signify 235
   Explaining Tenure To Parents Who Work
      for a Living 241

**Woodmont May Feel Free But Isn't:
Cost And Financial Aid**.......................... 248
   Our Cash-Only Policy........................... 254
   A Breakdown Of What Your $132,000 A
      Semester Pays For........................... 255
   Our Revised Policy Regarding "Free Tuition"
      QR Codes 259
   Posted In Over 50,000 Unisex Bathrooms 261
   Non-Academic Scholarships..................... 263
   Our No-Refund Policy 267
   Attend Classes Exhausted and Mentally
      Depleted: Work-Study Programs 268
   Why Our Textbooks Are So Expensive and
      What Little You Can Do About It............ 270

Life At Woodmont 278
   Construction Projects Around Campus and
      Why They'll Still Be Ongoing When
      Your Own Children Attend Woodmont 280
   The Place Where No One Goes:
      The Fourth and Fifth Floors of the
      Woodmont Art Museum 283
   You Might Recognize Us as the College Setting
      for *Sorority House Massacre 3: Naughty
      Nightmares*................................... 289
   Our $50 Million I.M. Pei Designed Indoor
      Wave Pool................................... 296

Chancellor's Letter

WELCOME FROM WOODMONT CHANCELLOR DUNCAN WELLS

Listen, I need half a million dollars now right now. You have to send it or it's all over, everything's over. You hear me? My whole life is going away if I don't get $500,000 in my bank account immediately. If you can't send it online, you can wire it from a Western Union or a check cashing place or probably from a convenience store. Jesus, I am so fucked. I'm sorry, Mary. I'm so goddamn—

WELCOME FROM WOODMONT CHANCELLOR CLAIRE SOTO

As Woodmont's new chancellor, it is my great honor to introduce you to the vibrant learning community you'll find at this prestigious institution. The following pages will provide you with an overview of everything Woodmont has to offer. By the time you're done reading, I'm sure you'll be as eager to be a part of the Woodmont community as I am. But, first, let's talk herbal libido supplements. Fact is, if you buy them from a chain store, you don't know what you're getting. That is why you should always purchase your testosterone boosters and other sex drive enhancers exclusively through a Certified Pleasure Ambassador such as myself. How do you know it's not a scam? I get that question all the time! To begin—

WELCOME FROM WOODMONT CHANCELLOR MICHAEL NGUYEN

Joseph Stalin's propaganda minister once said something wise but also quite funny—

"Education is the yard waste bag for the leaves of ignorance."

Woodmont *by the numbers*

14,000 STUDENTS *from all* **50 STATES**

except those 37 where Woodmont has agreed not to recruit in compliance with a class-action settlement in which Woodmont College continues to admit no wrongdoing nor unlawful conduct of any litigious kind.

500 FACULTY MEMBERS

honestly trying their very best in their disciplines, even if it doesn't always appear that way.

10

THE NUMBER OF LUXURY FRESHMAN DORMS, EACH WITH NO MORE THAN A MODERATE TO SEVERE RISK OF RADON POISONING OR CORONAVIRUS OUTBREAK.

Student to raccoon ratio: **3 to 1**

500–750 feet: Average distance between freshmen students and our lecturing adjuncts.

0 The word count of our policy towards illegal use of bath salts.

$2 BILLION: Cost of our state-of-the-art fitness center, previously known as the Jeffrey Epstein Foundation Woodmont Fitness Center and then, out of respect for alleged victims of the disgraced financier, subsequently renamed the JE Foundation Woodmont Fitness Center.

1,500 courses each term, more than 86 percent of which are assigned an instructor.

My favorite class is American Literature. I love how the adjunct Ms. Pulit teaches with a variety of materials and in a language (Portuguese) that I can't understand. It makes it that much more challenging and somehow more interesting. I feel sorry for Ms. Pulit because of what she's paid ($7 an hour) so I don't say anything.

MARC MOONEY
Junior

$97,000: Approximate annual damage to neighboring cities' cemeteries during visits from Woodmont athletic teams.

25: Number of "quiet" dorms for students who probably weren't going to lose their virginity until they were 25 anyway.

35: Number of minimum-security and conjugal-visit trailers for white collar offenders.

45: Number of luxury penthouse dorms for our Saudi friends.

Students who receive financial aid from Woodmont, including scholarships **(2%)** or half of a penny cut in two by a laser **(98%)** and framed for free.

4: Agreements with nearby universities allowing Woodmont students to use their dining halls during overnight hours while Woodmont's own dining facilities are bleached from top to bottom.

MAP KEY

1. That One Incredibly Ugly Building Leftover from the '70s
2. Coronavirus Testing Station (closed for bedazzling)
3. Mysterious Obelisk Construction Project (estimated completion: 2028)
4. Fraternity Row
5. Channel System Directing Bedbugs to Fraternity Row
6. Quad for Those Who Love to Blast Bob Marley
7. Faculty Body Modification Parlor
8. Center for Unnecessary Studies
9. Men's Lacrosse Fortress and Surrounding Moat
10. Statue of Confederate Soldier Made Less Offensive With "Hate Has No Home Here" T-Shirt
11. Admission Office and Afterhours Cash Deposit Drop
12. The Freakishly "Non-Traditional" Student Dorm
13. Panoramic Observation Deck for Controlling Parents
14. The Place Where No One Goes: Woodmont Art Museum
15. Microdosing Lounge
16. Dupont Dow Chemical Center for the Advancement of Environmental Studies
17. Hacky Sack Arena Built on Former Site of Indigenous Rights Land
18. Hard Rock Quantum Physics Bar & Laboratory Center
19. Warning! *Townies* Just Beyond This Point!
20. Pickle-Ball Courts for the Lazy and/or Unathletic
21. Post-Grad Life Virtual Reality Simulation Center
22. Our $75 Million, Pritzker-Award-Winning, Rem Koolhaas-Designed Trigger Warning Lounge
23. Post-Apocalyptic Desalination Plant, God Forbid
24. Woodmont Sweatshirt Superstore and Overpriced Book Annex
25. Rupert Murdoch Young Conservative Argument Chamber
26. Homeless '82 Woodmont Graduate Who Lives in a Pup Tent (*Avoid*)
27. Former Library Overtaken by Raccoons
28. Incense Repository

WOODMONT COLLEGE • Admissions Guide

37	Our $100 Million Frank-Gehry-Designed Titanium Safe Space
38	New Math Lab with Tons of Pricey Glass Floors and Columns
39	Former President's House (Now Divorced President's Ex-Wife's House)
40	President's One-Bedroom Garden Apartment
41	The Taco Bell Breakfast Crunchwrap Combo Quantum Computing Lab
42	Official Store for Van Gogh Prints, Keep Calm and Drink Beer Posters, and Close-Up Photos of Worn Ballet Shoes
43	Center for Unwatchable Black and White Swedish Film Studies
44	Smoothie King Memorial Chapel and Multi-Denominational Prayer Space
45	World's Largest FIFA Amateur Video Gaming Superdome
46	We're Not Sure. Map Is Too Small. Some Sort Of Niche Nontraditional Dorm For Freaks?
47	Liberal Arts Kiosk
48	Unexploded Mine
49	Faculty Parking Space
50	Sketchy Freestanding ATM
51	Center for Creative Arts + Phone-Charging Station
52	Short-Term Transfer Student Quarantine
53	Adjunct Stockade and Coronavirus Quarantine Center

29	Hazing Cemetery
30	Haunted, Sacrificial Cliffs of Belvedore
31	1960s Concrete Sitting Area and Now Skateboard Park
32	World's Largest Carbon-Neutral, Fossil Fuel-Free Building (Purpose Not Yet Determined)
33	Memorial of Racist Alumnus Senator Ebeneazer Truman
34	Library with Kick-Ass Spiral Staircase
35	Woodmont Fitness and Health Center, Previously The Jeffrey Epstein Foundation Woodmont Fitness and Health Center, And Now Just The JE Foundation Woodmont Fitness and Health Center
36	Student Health and Pubic Crab Elimination Center

WORDS: **JASON ROEDER & MIKE SACKS**
DESIGN: **DANIELLE DESCHENES**

BEN KAWALLER

Naked Homosexual Desert Caper

♦

When the world is in session, **Ben Kawaller** *makes funny videos for* **Los Angeles** *magazine and* **Wehoville***. He has alienated gay Republicans, witches, and men who like to have sex dressed as dogs.*

Shortly after I moved to L.A., I fell in with a group of self-described "nudies," an association of sexually permissive men who'd every so often get together to do various activities—hikes, barbecues, video gaming—naked. I don't myself identify as a "nudie," in that I do not ascribe any elevated meaning to the state of being naked; in fact, for all but a very small portion of my social interactions, I would much rather *not* be naked. This minor difference aside, though, I felt I could be a terrific asset to the nudie culture.

It was with high hopes that, one summer day, I decided to join thirty or forty nudies on a naked excursion to Deep Creek Hot Springs, which is somewhere in the Mojave Desert near San Bernardino. The Facebook-based invitation to the outing was, I noted, coyly averse to any overt sexuality. But I could read between the lines: what else could "a day of appreciating beauty" mean if not that I was in store for a mind-blowing outdoor gang-bang with my new best friends and future husband?

The plan was to carpool to the hiking spot, and we were to meet at the driver's place at 9 a.m. I'd realized the night before, however, that this timetable left little time after waking to have a fully satisfying spell in the bathroom, and in anticipation, I'd taken an overnight laxative. By 8:45 in the morning, though, it had yet to produce any results, and I left the house with a great sense of foreboding. I tried to put this matter out of my mind and focus on befriending my carpool companions.

The driver, Rick, was an impossibly hunky twenty-five-year-old with shaggy blond hair who held a genuine interest in surfing. We'd be riding in his SUV; we'd need four-wheel drive for this journey, the kind of rugged power a guy like Rick could provide. The other guy was an equally dreamy thirty-something who I realized upon greeting was my eye doctor.

I hugged them both hello, then started disrobing. Rick stopped me with an almost insulting urgency, then helpfully noted that we wouldn't be getting naked until we'd hiked down to the springs. I pulled up my pants and got in the car.

Now, I have nothing against gorgeous people, but I need a little less facial symmetry than Rick and the doc were sporting for me to behave like a normal human being. You'd think that in situations like these, when whatever beauty I have is neutralized by way of comparison, I'd try to mitigate things by turning on the charm. Instead, these seem to be

REACH INBOX HERO

PLAY THE EPIC EMAIL GAME

ADVENTURESNACK.com

only situations in which I am sufficiently petrified to assume an air of aloofness. So with Rick driving and Dr. Hynes in the passenger seat, I sat in the back, where I pretended to be uninterested in either of them and obsessed over when I might next see a toilet.

An hour and a half later, we arrived in the middle of a dusty, hot landscape that gave way to a winding and rocky trail that led down into a ravine. There did not appear to be a restroom for miles, aside of course from the vast open restroom that is the natural world. I was, I realized, a ticking time bomb en route to an orgy.

We started along the trail, the mid-morning sun already punishing. I soon fell into a reverie over the possibility of a future with Rick, despite his giving every indication of having a personality disorder. "I don't really care about other people," he'd confessed at one point, tossing his phenomenal hair and sending my loins into agony. "I think when you meet the right person you'll care," I said, affecting emotional stability. I would save him, beautiful antisocial Rick; he would come to love me, the man who would finally make him realize his capacity for basic empathy. He did not respond, having evidently lost interest in the conversation.

We finally reached the springs, where a growing contingent of nudies luxuriated on a sandy strip that lay before several natural pools.

"When do we have sex?" I asked my eye doctor.

"I think today is more about enjoying the scenery," he said, and I began to worry I'd made a terrible mistake.

I was in for another rude and sorry surprise at the base of these mountains: other people. Straight people. Now, in nearly all settings, women and heterosexual men are two of my favorite social groups, but they were a most unwelcome presence here. It didn't matter that they were also naked—they'd cast a decidedly asexual pall. Which meant that there were three dozen naked Los Angeles homosexuals at my disposal and hours to fill with…conversation.

I took off my clothes. It was the first time I'd ever been naked in public, maybe even the first time I'd been naked outdoors. I wish I could say I was overcome by some profound psychic shift, that I suddenly understood the brotherhood of…nudity? Mainly, I found it unnerving to be in a social setting without any pockets. I had never realized how much my pockets had soothed me until this day; I felt adrift without them. I asked around, but nobody else was having any pocket withdrawal. I was having trouble

HORSE DRAWN CARRIAGE

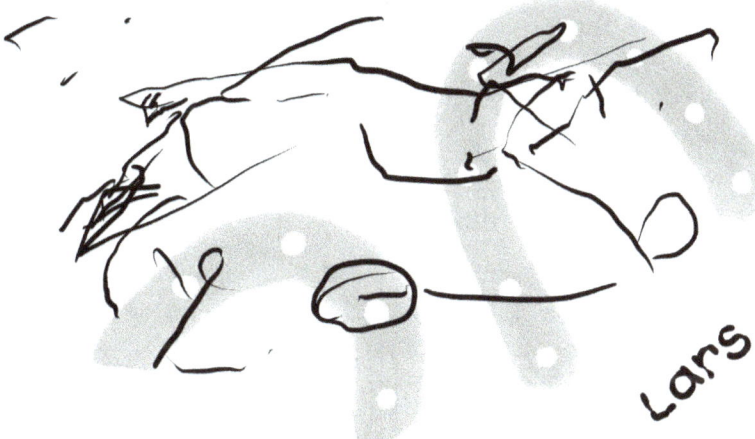

Lars

finding other topics of discussion.

I turned to two guys, a twenty-something who looked about fifteen, and a strong-jawed guy around my age, and remarked to the older one that his teeth, which were remarkably white, were remarkably white. He flashed me a smile that flipped my stomach and told me they were entirely fake, and for a moment I wondered how much trouble it would be to have all of my teeth knocked out and replaced with such an arresting set of veneers.

"What do you do?" I ventured.

"I'm in luxury real estate," he said. "What about you?"

"I'm a talent-agency hireling," I said, hoping to impress him with an SAT word. He did not seem floored by me.

I glanced at the kid, who was nonchalantly holding his leg behind his head. "What about you?" I asked.

"I'm an acrobat," he replied, and I hurled silent curses at the oblivious sunbathing heterosexuals who had ruined the afternoon.

I made my way down to the water, where Rick was attracting an audience. He had managed to get himself wedged into an inflatable circular tube he'd sat in, and he was now bent over and tottering around on the beach, feigning helplessness. Somehow, the naked men surrounding him were able to experience this display as a delightful bit of physical comedy, rather than as the visual torture it actually was, given that it seemed unlikely that Rick would be following up this routine by passing himself around for us all to molest. Certainly not with the goddamn cast of *Friends* forty feet away.

How much longer did we have to stay here? What was the appeal of nakedness without gratification? I was having the same feeling I get around go-go boys, whose job seems to be to alert everyone to the fact that they are not having sex with them. For that we pass out dollar bills? For this I schlepped across Judea?

Not willing to give up on the dream, I joined a subsection of the group and ventured off to another, more private beach that turned out to be free of humanity—now was surely the moment! But it was also the moment when I finally felt the visceral stirrings I'd hoped to induce before leaving the house that morning. I realized then that I had a choice between seeing how things panned out with this secluded cadre of naked boys…and doing what had to be done. Defeated by nature, I made my way back to the main camp, where I proceeded to dazzle the crowd with all the sexual vivacity that comes from asking around for a roll of toilet paper.

That procured, I started climbing up into the wilderness in search of a place to relieve myself. Though there was ample shrubbery, there seemed to be no spot that did not look down upon the beach. It seemed to me that should any of these nudies chance to train his eye on the hill behind them, he would surely spot me amidst the grandeur of nature,

Give your kid a book just for laughs.

When James Patterson teams up with Joey Green, something funny happens.

Not So Normal Norbert is a rollicking adventure into a futuristic world, where different is dangerous, imagination is insanity, and creativity is crazy!

Norbert Riddle lives in the United State of Earth, where normal means following the rules, never standing out, and being exactly the same as everyone else, down to the plain gray jumpsuit he wears everyday. He's been normal his whole life—until a moment of temporary hilarity when he does a funny impression of their dictator, Loving Leader . . . and gets caught!

Now, Norbert's been arrested and banished to planet Zorquat 3 in the Orion Nebula, where kids who defy the rules roam free in the Astronuts camp. Norbert has been taught his whole life that different is wrong, but everyone at Astronuts is crazy, creative, and completely insane!

"Readers will chortle at the relentless wordplay, a supporting cast made up almost entirely of caricatured grown-ups and young pranksters, and Norbert's winning mix of glibness and gullibility."—*Booklist*

Funny books turn kids into serious readers.

horrifically marking my territory. So I walked up and up, knowing that every step I took was a step farther from the whole reason I'd subjected myself to this harrowing pilgrimage.

This was very far from the scenario I'd envisioned when I'd pictured an afternoon of naked frolicking. I could hear the occasional peal of laughter from the people by the water, people who seemed genuinely to be enjoying themselves. Then, as if in jealous protest, I unleashed unto the earth an intestinal monstrosity as vile and wretched as any produced by man or nature, an unspeakable assault on all things good and holy, an atrocity whose very being seemed to confirm the bleakness of existence itself. The afternoon had reached a low point.

By the time I returned to the water, everyone was back on the main beach. "Was there an orgy?" I asked the acrobat.

"No," he said. "It doesn't always happen."

It was a small but welcome comfort to know that I hadn't missed out on group sex so I could go number-two on the side of a mountain.

But then—if not sex, what were these people doing with each other?

"We talked," said the acrobat. "Hung out."

I stared at him blankly, then asked for his number. Reaching for my phone, I found only my bare thigh.

The hike back up the mountain was more dispiriting than the hike down, given that the only possible intimacy waiting at the end was a car ride to civilization with Rick and my eye doctor. Stopping at the top, someone commented on the magnificent view. I turned to look down at the canyon we'd just climbed out of. Half-shaded by the afternoon sun, it looked far less scorched and dry than it had hours before, the rolling hills criss-crossing as they descended into shadow. Above us, like always, was the absolute blueness of our sky. The whole thing was, in fact, majestic. I hadn't noticed.

"Did you have fun?" Dr. Hynes asked as we buckled ourselves back into sturdy Rick's SUV.

"Not really," I told him, feeling I should be honest with my doctor. I probably should have said, "Yes, what a beautiful day!" But I didn't have the energy. Hiking is exhausting, and so is pretending to be an adventure-loving free spirit when all you want to do is lie down—preferably with someone else.

I am still not sure what the point of our sexless nudity was. I suppose that when you're stripped bare, there's an immediate intimacy you don't get in normal life. I wish I could say that, in such a state, I was able to open myself up to something beyond anxious small talk with a bunch of people with whom I likely had few things in common. I wish I could say that the nudies made me feel free, or "at one with nature," or like I was sharing in some fraternal bond. But I didn't feel any of those things. I just felt naked. B

"I didn't know you could finish Netflix."

What's So Funny About Peace, Love & Divorce Lawyers?

The Ultimate Cartoon Book on Love and Marriage

All's Fair in Love & War
THE ULTIMATE CARTOON BOOK

by the World's Greatest Cartoonists

Bob Eckstein, editor

Princeton Architectural Press

www.papress.com

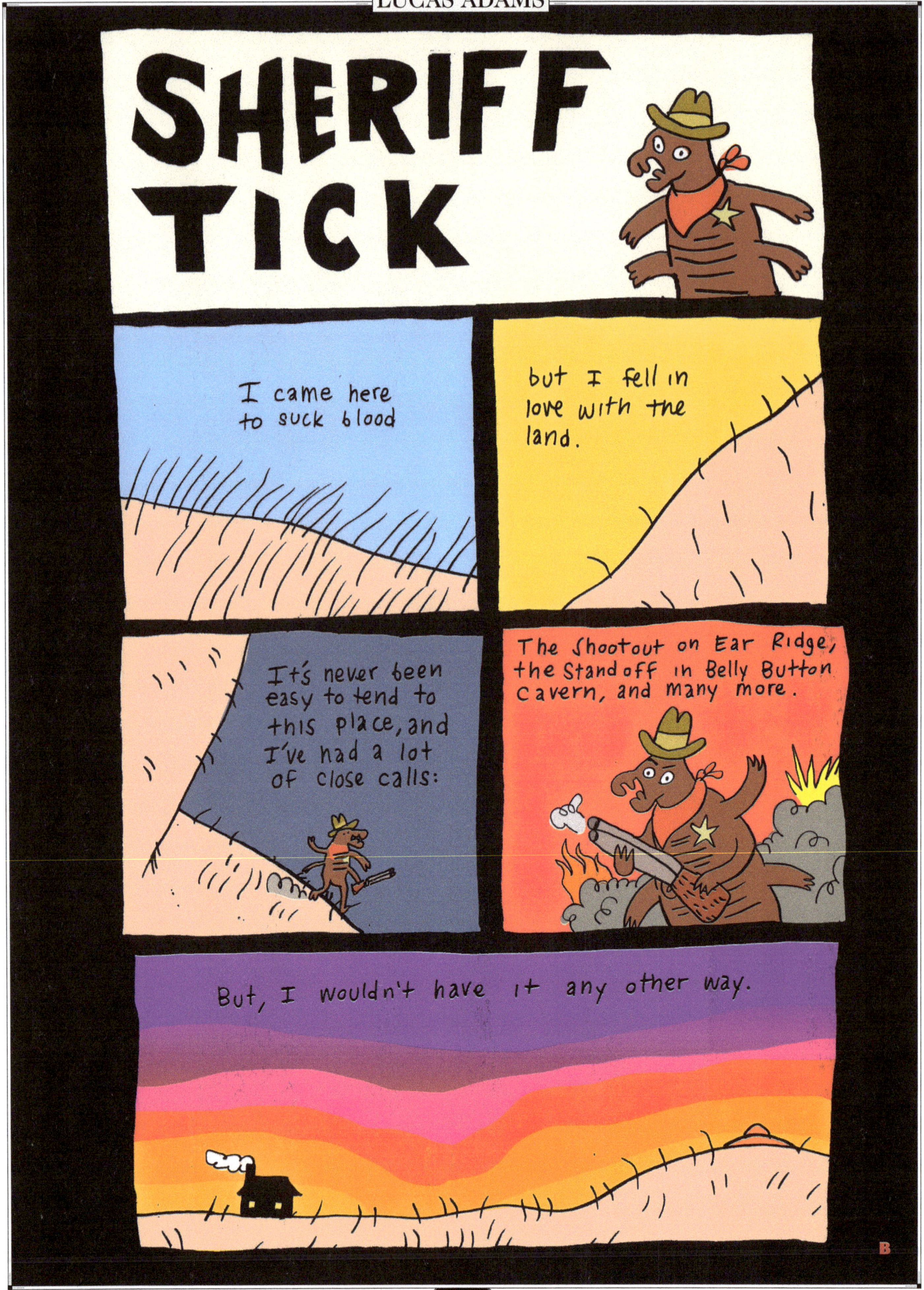
SHERIFF TICK
I came here to suck blood
but I fell in love with the land.
It's never been easy to tend to this place, and I've had a lot of close calls:
The Shootout on Ear Ridge, the Standoff in Belly Button Cavern, and many more.
But, I wouldn't have it any other way.

Harry Bliss & Steve Martin

THE PERFECT HOLIDAY GIFT FOR ANYONE (OR EVERYONE!) ON YOUR LIST

A WEALTH OF PIGEONS

A Cartoon Collection by acclaimed *New Yorker* cartoonist Harry Bliss and multi-talented comedian Steve Martin

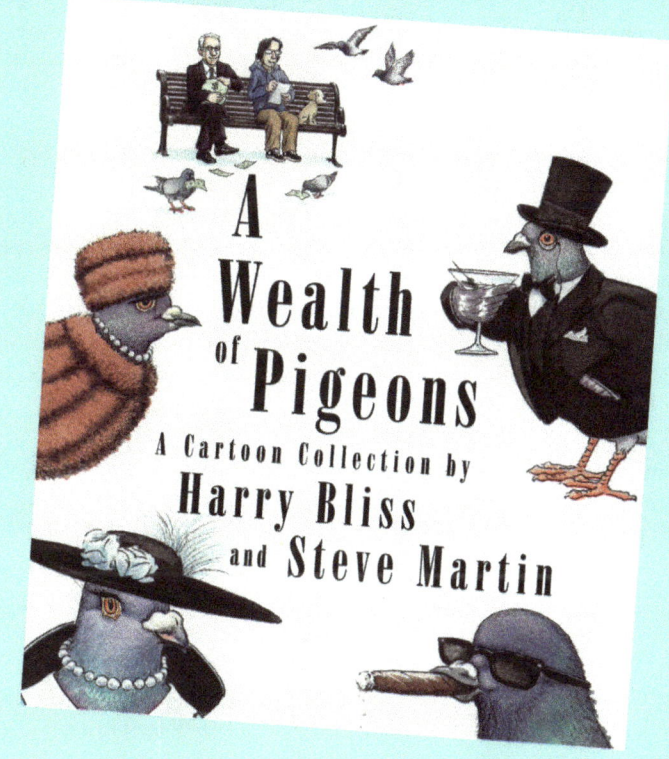

ON SALE NOVEMBER 17
AVAILABLE EVERYWHERE BOOKS ARE SOLD

CHRIS GALLETTA

Ike of the Foolsguard

Once upon a time I went questing into a dragon cave, which was not the kind of quest that best suited me. I'll be generous to myself and say I was terrified.

I was the runt of my siblings. The oldest, Barthem, was strong and hirsute and had no problem riding up to a row of cooing maidens with a handful of dogtooth or gillyflower. Our sister Grail, the middle child, had bucked the gender norms of the day and taken to the battle axe like a Flem to liver paste. They generally loved adventure and war and pillaging (the good kind) and testing the limits of their dumb luck. And so, a few days ago, to the shock of some and the surprise of none, they'd been captured by a dragon—the very dragon whose cave I was riding toward. (Did I say riding? I was on foot. The horses did not love me and seemed to bite the apples I fed them with a hint of bemusement.)

The cave was ghastly, its mouth lined with jagged black dolomite, sickly green and yellow geodes pocked into the walls like spider eyes. I don't know why I volunteered for this—oh wait, I do! Because Father said I had to volunteer, or else "even *more* shame" would befall our house.

I was training to be a jester, and that was not anyone's idea of how the son of a king should be spending his early manhood. Never mind that I actually liked it—thinking up jokes, crafting them by candlelight. And jesterdom wasn't entirely risk-free, was it? A moody lord and an ill-considered bit of political satire could be quite the combustible mix. Also, sometimes a tongue simply had to be cut out, and the jester's was usually all aflap.

Was it worth pointing out Father's double standard in celebrating Grail's "hard" hobbies but scorning my "soft" ones? Probably not; the last adviser who had lectured him about the patriarchy ended up smeared in goose blood and thrown to the bears.

I was barely a step inside the cave when a coterie of snake guardians slithered up, hissing their customary threats and temptations. I beheaded one of them with my dull sword, and it was an ordeal for both of us—more so for him, but I am just not a big "blood" guy.

The irony here was that I actually did want to be a hero. Sure, my siblings used to throw goblets of piss in my face—this would be where I'd say "but that was years ago" were it applicable—but they were also the only ones who supported my joining the Foolsguard, if tacitly and quietly. All three of us were on eggshells around Father, who had been even surlier lately since "allowing" mother to leave him for Lord Gallantjoust, who is said to have named himself.

As I skulked deeper into the cave, the path split in three. After my eyes adjusted to the gloom, I could just make out a dim orange light at the end of the leftmost tunnel, and thusly followed it. If luck was with me (spoiler: it never was), this would be one of those erudite dragons who spoke in rhyme and sat on its hind legs; the other kind just straight murdered you within seconds. Under the circumstances, I could deal with a little affectation.

Nearer the light, the walls glistened with a mysterious film, maybe dragon spit or some kind of glandular secretion—it all felt very lair-y. I turned the corner, and sure enough a deep green, tower-sized dragon had a cauldron on the boil. He was slicing some comically large peppers and onions, presumably from a dragon garden out back, or maybe from the underworld. Barthem and Grail were alive, but bound and hanging from the ceiling. The dragon was referring to a large cookbook, so this was definitely the twee, Anglo-literati type I mentioned.

Barthem saw me and I moved a finger to my lips. He

A former contributor to Letterman, **Chris Galletta** *wrote* The Kings of Summer *and is working on a stop-motion animated comedy. This is the most dialogue a dragon has had in any of his work to date.*

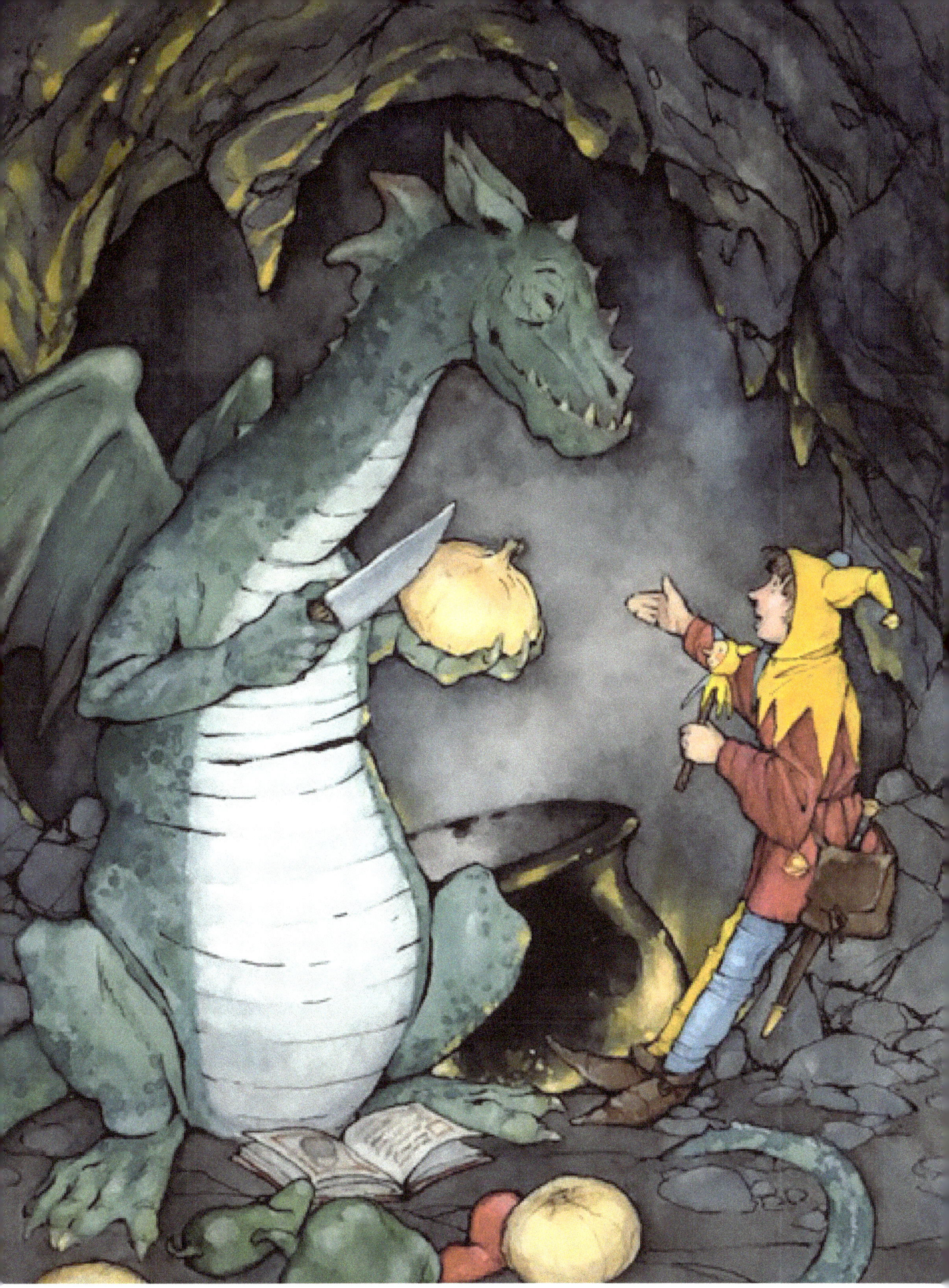

shouted, "Ike! Thank the stars!"

The beast turned, snarling: "Who be you? Where be thy king? Hath he no love for bartering?"

This was going to be exhausting.

"I'm Ike," I said. "I don't want to fight you, and I'm sure my siblings didn't either. There's just been some confusion. Perhaps we can talk this over like men of letters?"

"Bahh! I am no man!"

"No, no, I know," I replied. "'Men of letters' is just a common phrase, an idiom. I know that's not your species—I spoke carelessly, and I'm sorry."

My siblings rolled their eyes; they thought I policed my speech too much as it was, especially if I wanted to "get into comedy." I had some thoughts of my own on their speech, believe me.

The dragon said, "I'm Hectopol, the liege of death! *I smite you with my hellish breath!*"

He inhaled, and a fireball started forming in his throat behind the lizardy membrane—which reminded me of a joke I'd jotted down in my tattered jester's diary, stored in my official Jester's Satchel that every apprentice had to buy (so far mine contained a deck of trick cards and a cadaver's hand that I'd learned to have some on-and-off-the-record fun with): "Say, Hectopol—how do dragons weigh themselves?"

The dragon glared, ready to pop.

"With their *scales!*"

Hectopol arched a brow—then chuckled a bit, despite himself. As he did, the growing flame in his throat disappeared, a wisp of smoke escaping through his flared nostrils. Interesting.

The dragon puffed his chest again, this time slightly pissier. I tried another joke (these were first passes, let me stress): "Do you know which knight designed father's round table?"

The beast narrowed his eyes, weighing his desire for the punchline against his desire to kill me.

"Sir *Cumference*," I said.

Hectopol simmered—it was an execrable joke, I knew that—but then, to my exquisite relief, chortled. His throat-flame fizzled again; my sister Grail whom I love and was here to save shouted, "Ike! Stop telling your shitty jokes!"

As Hectopol readied his terrible mouthfyre for a third, and surely final, time, I searched my mind for a winner. "Two dragons walk into a tavern," I said. "One of them says, 'Is it hot in here, or is it me?'"

Hectopol shut his eyes and shook his head. He wanted no part of it.

"...Then the other dragon says, 'Why don't you take off your jacket?'"

Hectopol's lip quivered, he snarled and spit on the floor—and then barked out a genuine, hearty laugh.

I hopped upon the high rocks and cut Barthem and Grail down from their stalactites. We felt a rumble, and turned to see three, no, make that four dragons wandering into the cave, with the uncertain smiles of those suspecting they'd missed a good time.

"What's so funny, Hectopol?" said a red dragon with eyes as black as the soul of murder.

"Oh, the small spindly one told me a pretty good joke. Very dry with a good left turn at the end, sort of a frustration of the expectation of a punchline." The dragons nodded along, really dialed into the analysis. I didn't like intellectualizing humor that much, but there are a lot of schools of thought on that.

Reading the room with his usual expertise, Barthem snatched up his lance and shield. "For the kingdom of Moatland!" He charged Hectopol, who absently flicked him against a rock. Grail ran to claim her axe and said, "In the name of my Father, king of—" and a sort of midsized yellowish dragon looked down at her and said "Can you both stop it for a second?"

I pressed my hands together into a little cathedral and said, "I think I read somewhere that five dragons make a *minyan*. Can we...?"

"Yes, yes," Hectopol said. "Be thee gone and all that. Come back with a few more jokes sometime!" Then he turned to his brethren and said, "Okay, so two dragons walk into a tavern. It's hot, so they say to the tavernkeep.... shit. I'm messing it up."

A purplish dragon with craggy, obsidian teeth dripping blood said, "Take your time."

On the path home, Barthem kicked at some leaves. "You didn't bring our horses. This is a two-day walk. Thank you for coming, obviously." I nodded, though my mind had long since turned back to the Foolsguard. Would it be possible—or even worth trying—to explain to Father that my silly japes had done knightly work today?

Grail said, "We don't have our bows, either. Maybe we can scare the rabbits to death." Barthem replied, "Ike's about to ask why we can't just eat berries."

Maybe I was. Alas it all.

A limited edition of 25 Giclée prints on archival stock, 8" x 10", signed by R. O. Blechman and Nicholas Blechman, is available for $325, postage included. Inquire at ro@roblechman.com.

They'll go fast!

MICHAEL GERBER

Real Boy's Life

In February 1977, when I was nearly eight, my mother herded everyone into the banquet room of The Cheshire Inn and married my stepfather. It says much about that time and place that I couldn't tell you whether there was a church ceremony, but I certainly remember the party after. When the bride waits tables and the groom tends bar, their reception is an extension of the tavern—and so my parents' hitch-up was consecrated by all of the regulars from Llewellyn's, a Welsh pub in St. Louis' Central West End. The full story of that night is likely never to be revealed, least of all by me, who was sent home around 8:00, but I can tell you two things for sure: One, people who were young in the 1970s tell the rest of us about half of what really went on. And two, if you want a marriage to last, hire a blind piano player.

As Llewellyn's unofficial mascot, I knew the groom and liked him very much. In addition to being a heavy pour with the grenadine, Greg Gerber was young and fun-loving and had (has) a kind of swashbuckling side that I admire but entirely lack. To him, the whole world is a parking space, and tickets just the beginning of the conversation. After four decades of close, occasionally appalled study, I can tell you that this approach to life *works*. My Dad's various benign ruses are constant and deserve a piece of their own, but for the purposes of this one, know that I immediately recognized him as a rascal with a noble heart. When he decided he was *for* you, that was settled; what you needed, you would get, and what various authority figures didn't know, wouldn't hurt them.

So for a single mother with a degree in Studio Art and a kid with just a touch of cerebral palsy, this particular pirate was just what the orthopedist ordered. Which is not to say that his lifestyle didn't take its toll; I remember him ducking out of a double-parked car telling me, "If a cop shows up, look cute."

Shit like that *ages* a child.

Still: among males at least, there are certain similarities of temperament between a young twenty-two and an old nearly eight. These occasionally alarmed my mother, but immediately charmed me. While still a student, Dad had liberated some of Webster College's video equipment and smooth-talked his way into a job as the videographer for the ABA's St. Louis Spirits. Sitting courtside at those games ("this is my assistant"), or at the old Busch Stadium, sneaking down into a luxury box he had not paid for, or at a raggedy municipal diamond in Forest Park, drinking a Coke he'd fished out of someone else's cooler as he played third base for Llewellyn's Sluggards, I thought, "*This* is a guy I can work with."

He, apparently, felt the same way about me. First informally, then more seriously after his upgrade to husband, Dad began the task of turning me into a Real Boy. Until then I had existed mostly as an object of wonder and curiosity, a semi-mythological creature passed between a bevy of beautiful and intelligent art students too young yet to have children of their own. This was exactly as excellent as it sounds, and my only regret is that life will never be quite that good ever again.

"What do you mean, 'He can't tie his shoes?'" I heard my new father's voice say one morning before school. It made perfect sense to me; someone in my position had no need for such commonplaces, and indeed performing them for me seemed to give my beautiful friends pleasure. In return I showed gratitude, and made them laugh, and both parties left entirely satisfied. Surely Dad would see this, and life would go on as before.

As his heavy footsteps approached, I calmly put aside my Captain Klutz paperback, ready to explain How Things Were to the new guy. I swung my stiff legs off the bed and as Dad entered, I smiled with a quiet dignity. As much dignity as possible, given that both of my shoes were untied.

"You know what today is?" Dad asked, not supplying time for a witty response. "Today is the day you learn to *tie your goddamn shoes*."

We were at it for an hour. I don't think my fingers were the problem; I was becoming a Real Boy, and I didn't like the downgrade. Who would?

Before Dad entered the picture, summer vacations didn't exist. To Mom and me, the entire concept was alien; bills and obligations didn't take two weeks off, so how could you? When you were born, someone dumped 4,000 pounds of peanut butter on you, and you spent the next 70 years trying to claw your way out. It wasn't so bad, if you learned

☙

◆

Michael Gerber *is informally barred from the State of Wisconsin.*

The Old Salt on Gull Lake in 1979, scanning the water for Great Whites.

"I think I'll go type this up."

to like the taste of peanut butter, but taking a break was not an option.

Dad's attitude was different. Looking back now, I see that he didn't come from money, just security; but to us? It was a whole new world. I still remember him telling me about the summer (early college, it must've been) that he and some friends rented a place on Martha's Vineyard. "We painted houses for money, and spent a lot of time on the beach."

People *did* that?

"I remember once when I was swimming, I looked up and, way off in the distance, I saw a shark."

People *survived* that?

"What kind?" I asked. At age six, for reasons I still cannot fathom, I had read *JAWS* and was terrifically scarred by the experience. "Was it a Great White?"

"Maybe," Dad said, smiling.

"It wasn't a Great White," my mother said. They'd been married a year and half now, and we were driving from Missouri to Wisconsin, to spend a week with Dad's grandparents. Mom wanted me to make a good impression, and my fear of sharks was so great I had trouble showering. Wet skin plus closed eyes equaled utter terror. (I still can't swim in pools.) Over and over my mother said, "Michael, there are no sharks in St. Louis," but logic had nothing to do with it. My parents found my phobia a source of hilarity, when it wasn't an inconvenience. "Tell him it wasn't a Great White, Greg. He's going to smell like sauerkraut."

"It wasn't a Great White," Dad said, then looked at me through the rear view. "*Probably*."

"Don't scare him!" Mom said. "Not unless you want to stop."

"We just stopped two hours ago." That meant eight more to go, give or take, depending on the weight of my father's foot. I remember the drives as interminable. St. Louis to Gull Lake, Wisconsin, is only 627 miles, but sitting there in the back seat, we might as well have been traversing the Silk Road. I brought books and my *MAD*s, and a few cars—Dad had gotten me a Goldfinger Aston Martin the last time they went to New York—but the boredom hung heavy and stifling, like the July heat.

If I had to guess, we took that first trip in my mother's old orange Mazda, the one with the chewed-up backseat. Two months earlier, Dad had left our dog Gus in the car during softball practice. It was only 70 degrees, and the windows were cracked, but Gus was furious. He could see what everyone was doing out there—running, jumping, chasing balls, all the stuff he really excelled at—and yet *he* was stuck inside the car. Gus vented his righteous fury with two solid hours of barking, punctuated by vicious attacks upon innocent upholstery. I was sent several times to give Gus water from a bottle tipped through the vent-window, but was too short to see the carnage he was wreaking. When Dad and I returned, the back seat of the car was filled with ragged chunks of beige foam and shredded black pleather.

Reader, I might have once been a semi-mythological creature, but not on my best, handsomest, most charming day could I have talked my way out of that one. And yet Greg did.

So Mom was clearly crazy about him. And also? She always rode in the front seat. There in the back, you were practically sitting on bare metal. And sharing space with luggage. On the other hand, the cooler was under my left hand. I'm not made of stone, you know?

"Are you drinking another Coke?" Mom asked. "That's your last one."

"That *is* the last one," I said, springing the Aston's ejector seat and sending the little plastic man pinging off the dome light. Then, a thought: "I need to pee."

"Aw, Mike, c'mon!" Dad said. "We're finally making some time!"

"Seriously?" Mom asked me.

"Would I lie to you?"

When Mom laughed, I knew I had won. "Greg, pull over," she said.

Dad did so, deeply unhappy. "Bring the bottle. I'm going to teach you something." Real Boy stuff.

Turns out that an eight-year-old penis fits perfectly in the neck of a Coke bottle. It took me a minute or two to get the timing right— Wait, wait, wait… LET 'ER RIP!—but we didn't have to stop again after that.

"Can I pour it out the window?"

"Don't you dare!" Mom yelled.

"Dad! Push the button for oil slick!" I yelled.

Dad laughed; I poured; Mom dreamed of a daughter.

As the child of an until-recently single parent, I prided myself on my flexibility; there was no adult I couldn't charm, and no situation I couldn't conform to. But being at Gull

Lake threw me. For one thing, George and Peg Anderson liked mornings. I... do not. Then, as now, I awake braced for impact. The cortisol doesn't recede before 10 a.m. at the earliest, and the idea that one would do anything, much less anything important, before midday—before you've gotten a chance to hunt for threats, before the day has declared its intentions—strikes me as asking for trouble. Which mornings provide in abundance, because mornings are when Morning People are out doing important Morning Things, like knocking on the door for rent or diagnosing your X-ray or asking what all that noise was last night. Think about all the worst experiences of your life; most of them happened in the morning. When I was a kid, all of my doctor's appointments were in the morning, and they usually hurt. All my surgeries were at the crack of dawn; I'm 51 now, and still wake up expecting someone to come at me with a scalpel. Mornings are, at best, the time you get through after the night before.

Not at Gull Lake; there the mornings began early and lasted forever. I swear to God, it felt like four minutes after midnight when I'd first hear Nan puttering around the kitchen, getting breakfast ready. At the first clank of a pan or gush of water from a faucet, my eyes would snap open, and I would lay there in that awful gray light, instantly flooded with dread. Then I'd hear Pop turn on the shower, and I would think: *Here we go again.*

Who were these people, apparently unaccustomed to ill fortune, for whom "the day was for the taking?" Among the birches and the blue, blue sky, the chipmunks and the ducks and the loons, we'd eat a hearty breakfast, then head off into the bright sunshine, off to pick berries, or hike, or head into Hayward to buy fudge. Almost as if nothing bad was waiting for us. The confidence of these people. The hubris. It was barbaric.

And yet...it seemed to work for them. About twenty years earlier, Nan and Pop had purchased this house, a former Boy Scout camp. This alone was a shocker; growing up in my mother's Irish Catholic family, the idea that any adult would've somehow accumulated enough money to buy property was fantastical. The only wealth we possessed glittered dimly from the past, an ironic plot point. "Peggy's husband had money. But then, the first week they were married, Something Happened. So she called from Chicago and said, 'Daddy, come get me.'"

In Mom's family, "So-and-So had come into a little money" was a set-up, leading to a punchline like "Then a firework went off and hit him in the eye." Wealth was not to be wished for. It was a complication, a test. It revealed character flaws, it caused regret. This story had been told by our people for one thousand years, beginning with the Viking longboats.

Nan and Pop—and I mean this in the nicest way—were those Vikings. Tall, strong, still vigorous in their late 60s, they were so Scandinavian that theirs was a mixed marriage—he was Swedish, she was Norwegian. (That's true; the families actually did fight.) They were so Scandinavian that they ate lutefisk. They were so Scandinavian, Nan dated Johnny Weissmuller...and turned him down because *he* wasn't Scandinavian. And because they were so Scandinavian, Gull Lake was not lavish; it was a lodge, a utilitarian staging area for adventures had outside. I remember a lot of blonde wood-paneling. All the furniture had scratchy upholstery; it was fine to sit on, but lying down on it hurt your face. Lying down was for bed, at bedtime, and nowhere else. On the walls there were paintings of ducks, and slightly rude Swedish phrases rendered in cross-stitch by my new grandma, when she was a girl.

Looking back, I realize now Gull Lake was beautiful. The lodge was surrounded on all sides by dense birch forest, and even on the sunniest days the house stayed dark and cool. Birdsong was constant. Every evening, we'd troop out to the patio for cocktail hour, peering out at the shimmering lake through tall trees as the loons called and the sun went down. Occasionally, a distant motorboat thrummed. If we were lucky, a chipmunk would come and eat birdseed out of Pop's hand. They'd never do that for me, no matter how much coaching I got. Their little expressions were clear: "You're not a Real Boy. You're a grownup pretending."

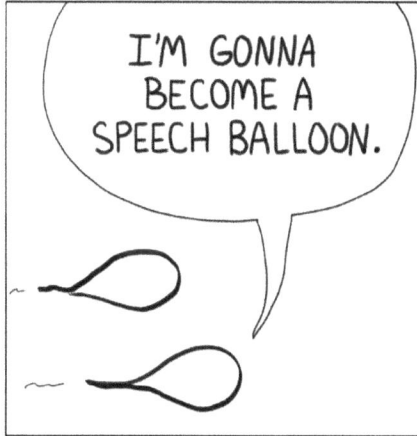

I was not an easy houseguest. It's not that I wasn't cheerful and polite; Mom had raised me properly. I helped out whenever asked, always ate everything on my plate, and was game for whatever was planned. It's just that I was an extremely verbal, high-strung eight-year-old with legs that didn't work well. Nan and Pop didn't know what to do with me. I didn't know what to do with myself.

Gull Lake had hosted generations of Real Boys eager for adventure in the woods and water. That was not me. Being on such shaky terms with the physical world, I was primarily interested in not dying—woods were a place to get lost, water a place to drown. There was no TV to speak of, and if there had been, staying inside would've been frowned upon. As a form of self-improvement, reading was marginally more acceptable, but Nan and Pop were not readers—once you'd flipped through the Field Guides to This or That, and learned the history of Ducks Unlimited, all that was left was the warning tag on your life jacket. Dad was smart enough to bring a Ludlum every year, but *he* was reading that; and I wasn't really interested in borrowing Mom's *My Mother, My Self*.

Besides boring old natural beauty, the house's only amenity was a decaying concrete basketball court. But basketball alone isn't very fun, especially if you're short, have a three-inch vertical, and missed as often as I did. 85 percent of my time was spent chasing rebounds through the underbrush, putting my hands into active spiderwebs and praying the ball wouldn't head down into some leafy crevasse too deep for me to climb out of. Then as now, my perfect vacation is one where I don't have to scream for help.

Picking raspberries was much more my speed for three reasons: 1) small chance of death; 2) raspberries; and 2) my mania for accumulation. Even today, I love to watch sports primarily to count everybody's yards and points; over my three trips to Gull Lake, picking berries became just short of a mania. Finally, something outdoorsy that I was good at!

Once every visit, Pop would declare that today was the day for berry-picking. He would then drive us all to a farm nearby, where I would look at the field of bushes like a general surveying terrain. Each of us would be given a capped plastic milk jug from which the bottom had been cut, and to which a strap had been affixed. This meant you could hold it by the handle—but professionals such as myself would wear it around the waist. Hands now free, I'd scurry among the brambles, deftly reaching between the thorns to pluck out the biggest, juiciest berries, ones even the birds couldn't get.

To walk into a field empty-handed, and leave an hour later with a gallon of raspberries—that was some serious Real Boy shit. I suddenly understood why the Vikings took their trips. The thorns of the raspberry bushes exacted a toll, but as any Norseman would tell you: What's plunder without a little blood?

We took three trips to Gull Lake, 1977, '78, and '79, and the experience taught me something very important: I prefer cities. In a state of nature, without sidewalks or asphalt, about every ten steps I catch my toe on something and sprawl. I can trip over almost anything: a rock, a tree root, a wadded-up Kleenex. I kid you not, I've tripped over a shadow.

Which is why I like boats.

Luckily, there was a boat at Gull Lake. It was a dented, peeling, twelve-foot aluminum skiff powered by a temperamental Evinrude, owned by some people who lived in a little house on the shore below. Year-rounders, they weren't exactly friendly—in fact, I only saw them once—but after years of currying favor (blocks of fudge from Tremblay's Sweet Shop) Nan and Pop had been granted some limited use of the rust-crusted craft. Dad and I would take it around the lake for a spin. Sometimes we'd fish, but there were better spots for that, stocked ponds or, if you wanted a challenge, places where muskellunge of mythical size and toothiness had recently been spotted. Gull Lake wasn't really for fishing, and was certainly too cold to swim. But it was almost achingly scenic, and tooling around called to me.

From the first time Dad and I went out together, I was determined to drive that boat. I knew there were no Great White Sharks in Gull Lake—*probably*—but still, it seemed safer somehow to be the driver of the boat rather than its passenger. If you hit the waves crosswise at any speed, the bow would buck wildly, sending shudders throughout the metal; I remember my small fingers gripping the edge tightly as we galumphed through the spray, both of us yelling with delight, hoping the damn thing would hold. I never got close to falling overboard, but to be safe I always wore an orange Mae West that the owners kept near the dock.

That first year, I was strictly ballast, a passenger. During the second, near the end, my dad started the engine, then said, "Come back here."

"Why?" What Real Boy test was being sprung on me?

"Just come back here. I don't want you to get all in your head." Dad was holding the tiller. "Put your hand on top of mine." The vibration of the engine through my hand, the smell of the gas and oil—intoxicating. (I am, though few people know this, a bit of a gearhead.)

"Now," Dad said, "when I move my hand away, grab the stick *tight*. You gotta keep the throttle turned all the way, or the engine's gonna die and we'll be out here for an hour."

With a cough and a sputter, we made the switch. My hand was small enough that it took some effort to keep the throttle twisted open, but I bore down, and ignored the pain Real Boy–style. Dad galumphed to the front of the boat, and it shook alarmingly. When it settled he said, "See the cabin?"

I didn't, but I didn't want Dad to think twice about letting me drive. "Yeah."

"Then take us home."

I was in heaven—so often immobile, I was moving freely, and fast; always under the control of others, I was finally in charge. When we got about fifty feet from shore, Dad and I switched places again, and he piloted us into the dock; at a certain point, you had to flip a switch and kick the languid engine into reverse, and I wasn't ready for that. But in general, I drove the boat deftly and well, loving every minute. When Dad took the picture on page 59, he had to order me not to smile.

The next year, our last year, I drove the boat constantly. I'd keep Dad out on the lake for hours, taking long detours that he'd complain about but have to put up with because, on a boat, the captain's word is law.

Finally, on the last night, I got up to do our usual switch. It was well past dusk—I'd pushed it—and there was just a sliver of light left. As the boat bobbed on soft swells, Dad said, "Hold on a second." He peered through the gloom. The cabin next to the dock was dark; the boat's owners had turned in for the night.

"Think you're ready to dock it?"

"I *know* I'm ready," I said. (Confidence has never been a problem.)

"Now listen: these people are really tight-assed. So if you think you can't do it, just flip the switch over to neutral, and I'll take it in."

"I won't have to," I said. "Piece of cake."

"Okay," Dad said. "Aim for the light at the end of the dock…

"Good…

"Good…

"You're coming in a little fast…

"Mike, you're a little fast!

"Mike! Flip it into reverse!"

"Neutral?"

"No! Reverse! FUCK!"

I did flip the switch, reader, I swear. Looking back, I think I flipped it too much—I slid the little tab over into neutral, but then when the boat didn't go backwards immediately, I flipped it back again, thinking I'd made a mistake. Perhaps? The details are a matter for the Naval Inquiry. All we know *for sure* is that the boat slammed into the end of the dock with a terrific BANG. This is without doubt the loudest sound ever recorded on Gull Lake, or in Wisconsin, or perhaps anywhere ever. It sounded like I'd knocked a hole in the lake itself.

Forward momentum stopped, the boat lurched sideways, torquing a divot into the crumbling wooden dock. I yelped in terror, whipping my hands away from the suddenly Satanic Evinrude. Bucking and yawing, the boat ground against the dock, making a terrible scraping groan.

Naturally, I tried to flee.

"STAY DOWN!" Dad ordered, launching himself towards me. The engine, usually so desultory, roared; the dock heaved, and for a moment it seemed like—in defiance of all natural and maritime laws—both the dock and the boat would sink, and Dad and I would end up at least wet and very possibly dead. Out of the corner of my eye, I saw a Great White shark. That part I am certain of.

The entirety of the chaos couldn't have been more than five seconds, but it felt much longer, like puberty or a kidney stone. A boundary had been crossed. When Dad finally shut off the engine, everything was quiet. Off in the distance, a loon called. Could we have gotten away with it?

And then the porchlight went on.

Two Gerbers spoke as one: *"Oh, shit!"*

Okay, now: what would a Real Boy do? He'd tie up the boat, just like normal. I clambered onto the half-sunken dock, but the piling was splintered all to hell. I mimed attaching the plastic rope; as it fell uselessly back into the water, a man appeared on the porch. With a shotgun? No, thank God—but I think I caught a glimpse of a poker. Or an ax.

A familiar smile crept across Dad's face. "Okay, Mike," he whispered out of the corner of his mouth, "look cute."

> "Stan Mack shows that a man can be as caretaking as a woman, and a woman can be as brave, funny, and loving in death as in life. This compassionate, irresistible memoir is a gift to all of us."
> **Gloria Steinem**, author, *Moving Beyond Words*

JANET & ME

An Illustrated Story of Love and Loss by
STAN MACK

Available now
at Amazon, Powell's or at your local booksellers.

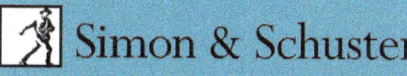

HARRISON SCOTT KEY

The Old Man With No Pants

(It is not as disgusting as it sounds.)

There is an old man who comes into the coffee shop, and he wears no pants. I see him at least once a week, and more frequently in the summer, when life for the pantless is more accommodating. He is a large man, and must be nearing eighty. His face is leathery and worn out, like the fissured leather of a European sedan purchased many years ago. His skin is purple and red, the color of a maturing bruise. It is hard to tell his race. Many years ago, I like to believe, he was a white man.

And also he is very, very tall. Unlike other old men, his legs are not the color and texture of overhead spackling, and they are not hairless. The legs are as blushing as the rest of him, and covered in red hair. It is not as disgusting as it sounds. He is not a disgusting old man. But he does resemble an aging and emaciated Sasquatch. He wears the same outfit every day: a tall blue baseball cap pulled down tight enough to touch the tops of his large square eyeglasses, brown loafers, and an ancient blue T-shirt draped over his aging skeleton, and also: his underwear. This is what I mean when I say he has "no pants." Because he doesn't have any on.

He also carries with him a small notebook and a pen, and he comes to the coffee shop, apparently, to write. It is a noble gesture for a man with no pants, and he is making a statement about other people like him and what they should feel free to do. So often, people with no pants are doing unwise things. I have seen people with no pants being arrested, or running down the middle of the street on their way to certain death. I have seen children in their underwear who have nothing better to do in their pants than poop in them.

Of course, at some point or another in the course of a day, all of us are without pants, but only in private, and almost never while wearing nothing but loafers. Which is to say, it can be quite frightening to walk around, even behind the impenetrable sanctity of your own four walls, wearing a top, but no bottom. If you do not understand me, I suggest you try it right now. Go home and dress yourself: shirt, socks, shoes, briefs, perhaps a sport coat to dignify the exercise – but leave out the pants. Now walk around. It is quite possible that your body will find this state of affairs enjoyable. It will want to leave the house. Your heart will be telling you, "It's okay to leave. This feels good. This feels right." But your faculties will interrupt: "Something is missing."

This is why we invented mirrors. To keep people from being too comfortable when leaving the house. The most comfortable costume I could imagine wearing right now would be nothing at all. Perhaps a quilt, with a belt to keep it from dragging. I love being naked, not because I am proud of my body, but because I feel like it needs to be aired out on a regular basis, the way you do with tents. It is a humane act—brave,

---

Harrison Scott Key *(@HarrisonKey) won the Thurber Prize for* **The World's Largest Man**, *the true story about what it's like to be related to insane people from Mississippi.*

Harrison Scott Key, photographed in Savannah, Georgia, in June 2020. Photo by **B.A. VAN SISE**.

even—to let myself be naked on occasion, an act of gratitude to my body for being willing to be a part of my life.

But I am also grateful to society, which is why I wear pants when I go outside. I am not calling the old man with no pants an ingrate. I am only saying that perhaps he has no mirror.

A month or two ago, I found myself walking around the house in a shirt. And that was all. It felt quite natural, I must say. Like when you have a picnic and you ask your lover, "Why don't we do this more often?" That's what it was like, my nakedness. My three young offspring darted hither and yon. The three-year-old stopped, looked me up and down, and ran away screaming.

"Your condition is upsetting the children," the wife said.

She refuses to say the word "nakedness." It's like Jews and Yahweh. She fears the power of my nudity, believes that she must hide herself in the cleft of the rock as my glory passes before her. I sat in a chair, still wearing only the T-shirt. Usually, the pantless are in a hurry to find clothing, but in the sanctity of my estate, I felt the desire to read. My five-year-old walked up and pointed a finger-gun at my vitals. "Put some pants on, cowboy," she said.

From bestselling author **MIKE REISS** comes a story of unlikely friendship between two very different animals.

AVAILABLE NOW!

"Humorous and deep."
—KIRKUS REVIEWS

"It becomes clear that some things, from buildings to friendships, just take time."
—PUBLISHERS WEEKLY

"A great addition to any parent, teacher, or librarians' collections."
—CM: CANADIAN REVIEW OF MATERIALS

HARPER
An Imprint of HarperCollinsPublishers
ART © 2019 ASHLEY SPIRES

These nude moments go unremembered as I sit in the coffee shop and judge the old man for wearing no pants. I know not whether he buys coffee or tea, but I am sure that he has no place to put his money. Still, he walks in, walks up to the counter, walks away with a small paper cup. Maybe it's just tap water, I reasoned, but then I saw it steaming. Steam costs money. Perhaps he is a magician, with the ability to conjure coinage out of thin air, or a thin column of steam.

These underwear, they're navy blue. Some days, maroon. They are knit briefs of the thinnest cotton material, as weightless as tissue paper, hanging limply over his octogenarian groin. The last time I saw someone wear underwear in public, those someones were girls, and I was in college, and I found their decision courageous, progressive, riveting. These coeds had cleverly sewn the flies shut and wore the napkin-thin garments as shorts.

"You go, girl," I said to them. And they did.

But the old man is not a coed, and his purplish legs are utterly twig-like, and where his backside should be, there is simply nothing. It is concave, as if his bottom had been removed during emergency surgery in the war, or accidentally left at the house, like one forgets a hat. I try not to stare. But I do. And do you know what it looks like? It looks like he's hiding a little kitten in there. It is a horrible notion, so early in the morning. It puts one's own nakedness into perspective.

Put some pants on, cowboy!

Also: He wears a thin gold chain, the *coup de grâce* in my attempt to categorize him in any Aristotelian sense. I cannot understand the desire of a man to wear a gold necklace unless he sells narcotics or works in a kiosk. I try to imagine him doing both and cannot, although I suppose he would be perfectly suited to standing behind a kiosk, which would shield the world from his kitten. After buying his coffee, he takes both newspapers from the rack, the *Savannah Morning News* and the *Times*. He reads the front pages and puts them back rather neatly and gingerly on the rack, so he doesn't have to pay, and then he writes. He sometimes sits outside, sometimes inside, and always in his underwear. Nobody says a word.

I wanted to dislike him, frankly. It was quaint at first, those many months ago, when I considered that in this Modern Age, a man can leave the house with no pants and his only concern out in the world is where to sit. But now, nearly a year later, I wanted the world to rise up with me and confront him. We needed to help him. We needed to come together, do something, give him a bathrobe or a quilt. I believed him to be insane.

Last week, the old man leaned down in front of me and said, "Excuse me?"

I expected his voice would be as cracked and broken as the skin stretched across his face. Mean and crazy old men tend to have mean and crazy voices. But his voice was as light and airy as he must have felt in his outfit.

"Pardon?" I said. He stood over me. I looked up at him.

"Would you happen to know when the Home Depot opens?" he asked, quite politely, a real gentleman, his voice a buttery tenor. No, not buttery. Lighter. Frothy. If I had closed my eyes, I might have thought it was a turtlenecked Robert Wagner asking.

I looked at my watch. It was 5:45 A.M., and his kitten was at eye level. "They open at six, in a few minutes," I said.

"Thank you," he said, as gently as one can hope for in a world like this, and he folded his jacket over his arm. He was carrying a windbreaker. It was a cool morning, and it heartened me to see he owned a jacket. It gave me hope that he would tie it around his waist. And then he left, maybe to go buy a new shovel or some lumber or a box of nails. I imagined him wearing a tool belt. The image lodged itself in a corner of my brain, where it remains.

I wanted to ask him, "Why are you wearing no pants?" But I'm glad I didn't. I no longer want to know. My brief conversation with him was civil, the kind of exchange on which one might construct a whole society. And that's enough for me. In the end, men remain hidden from one another, no matter how little they're wearing. Perhaps he will tell us his story one day. Perhaps that's the purpose of the little notebook. Perhaps he'll get to it, after a visit to the Home Depot. And then to Penney's. They really do have some great sales. B

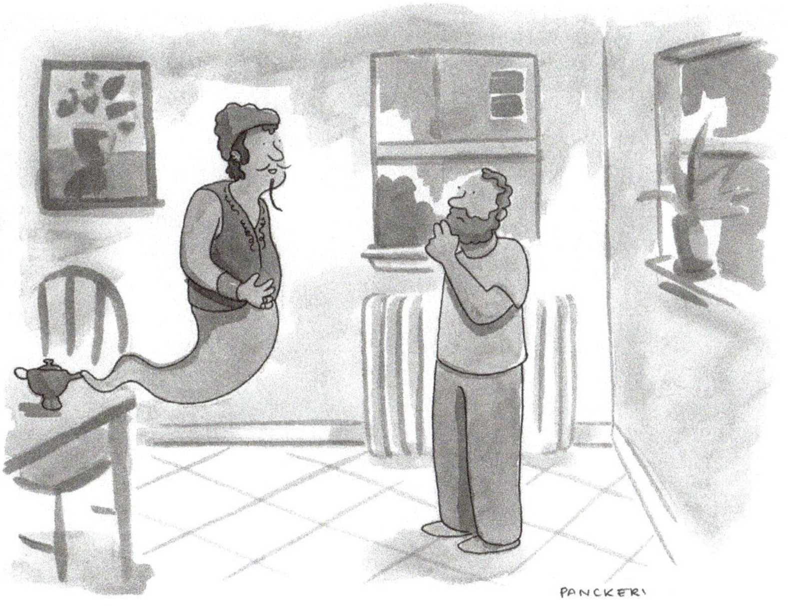
PANCKERI

"Well, I know what I'd *wish for—but you already have a lower torso."*

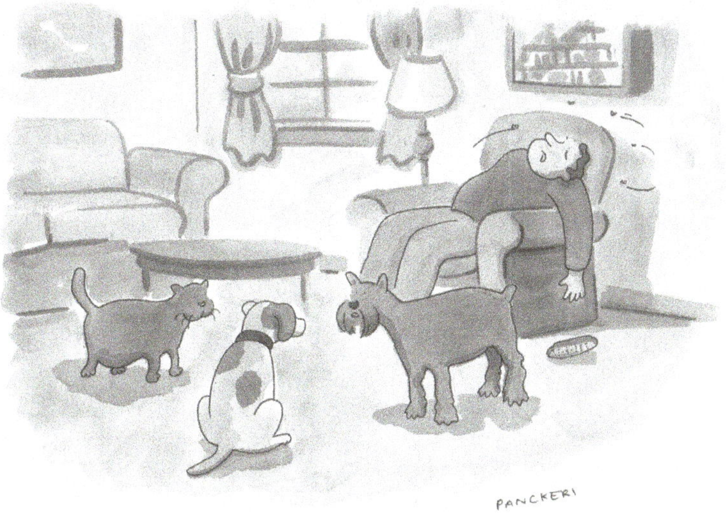
PANCKERI

"All in favor of eating just a little bit *of Bob, say aye."*

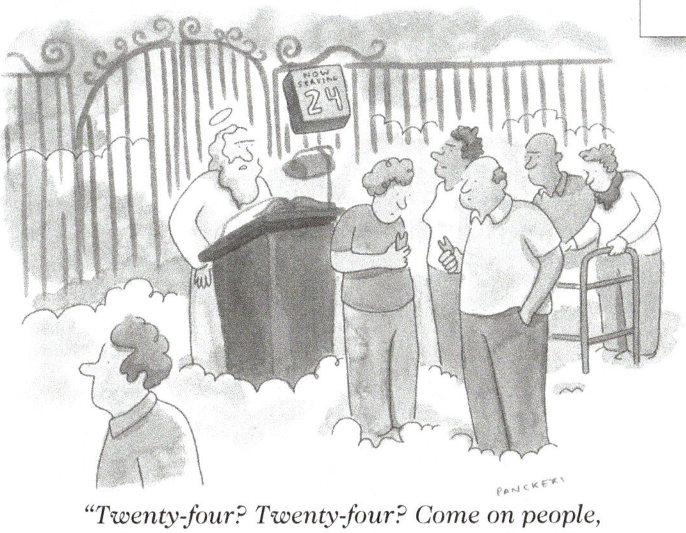
NOW SERVING
24
PANCKERI

"Twenty-four? Twenty-four? Come on people, does anyone have number twenty-four?"

ED SUBITZKY

The people you pass on the street...
What They're Thinking

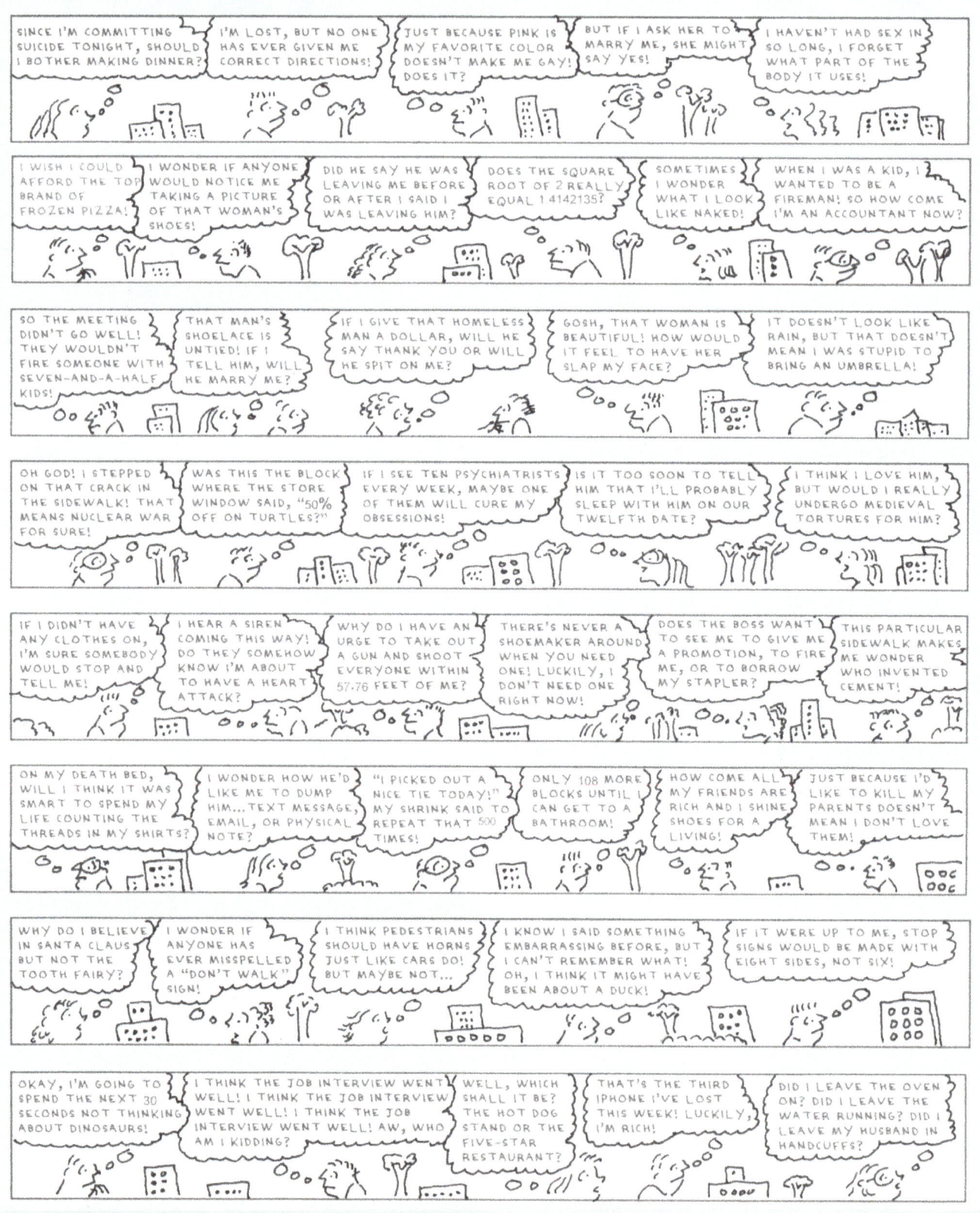

New from ROZ CHAST and PATRICIA MARX

ON SALE NOW

Falling in love is easy. Agreeing about how to load the dishwasher is hard.

You Can Only Yell at Me for One Thing at a Time: Rules for Couples is an illustrated collection of love and romantic advice from *New Yorker* writer Patricia Marx with illustrations by *New Yorker* cartoonist Roz Chast. This is the Valentine's Day and anniversary gift that couples have been waiting for. Available everywhere books are sold.

CELADON BOOKS

CeladonBooks.com/bookshop

THESE COLORS WILL MAKE YOU FEEL HUNGRY
FIND A UNIQUE RESTAURANT EXPERIENCE
IN JOHN DONOHUE'S NEW BOOK

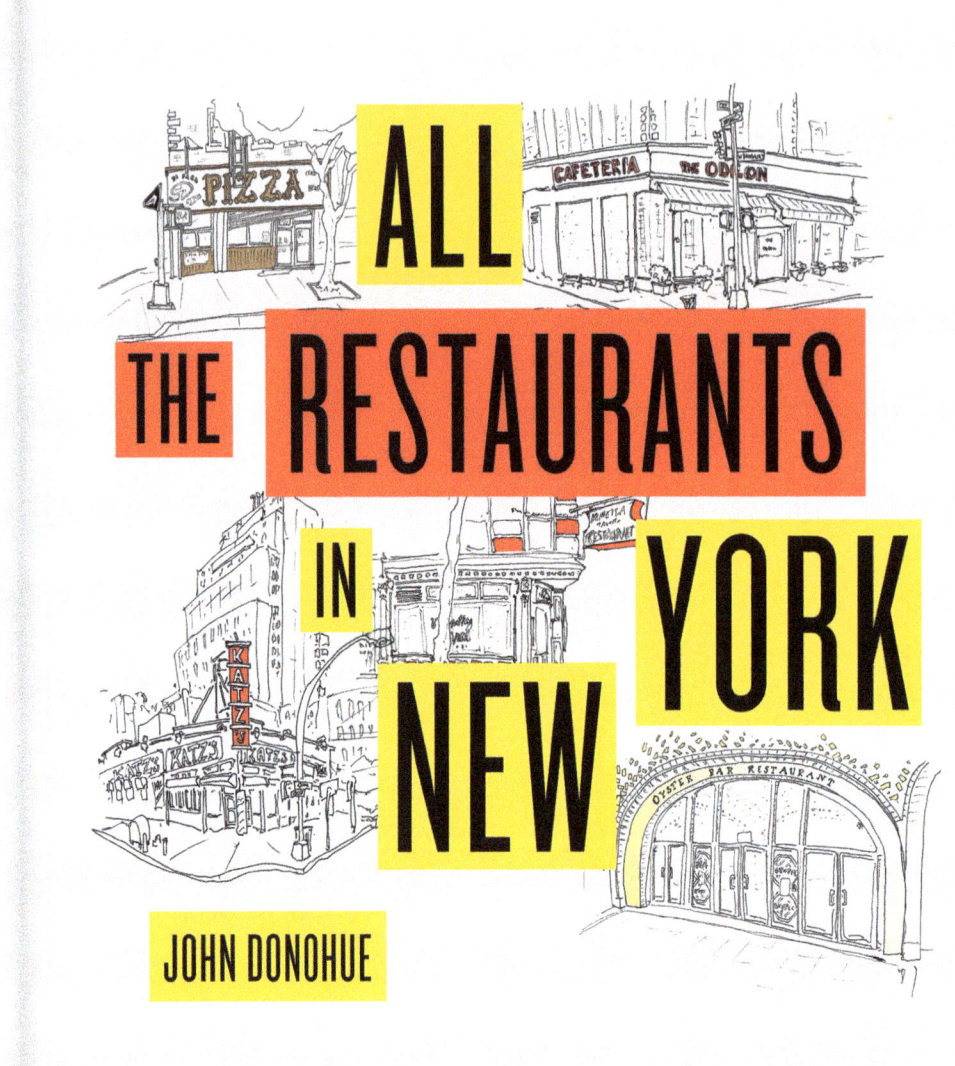

"John Donohue is the Rembrandt of New York City's restaurant facades."
—**Adam Platt**, restaurant critic, *New York* magazine

"If you know someone who's wild for a special New York restaurant, this is the perfect present."
-**Ruth Reichl**

Includes *that* Italian restaurant that brings in grandmothers from around the world to cook!

Available in fine bookstores everywhere
Find signed, limited-edition prints at alltherestaurants.com

OUR BACK PAGES

NOTES FROM A SMALL PLANET

The love that dare not meow its name • By Rick Geary

ONE DAY SHE JUST SHOWED UP AT MY DOOR.

HER ANTICS WOULD KEEP ME AMUSED FOR HOURS ON END.

SHE WAS HAPPY TO EAT THE SAME FARE EVERY DAY.

IN TIME SHE GREW INTO A BREATHTAKING CREATURE.

SHE COULD BE FIERCELY LOYAL AND PROTECTIVE.

IN FACT, SHE RIPPED TO SHREDS ANY FEMALE WHO CAME NEAR ME.

WHAT COULD I DO BUT MARRY HER?

OUR FAMILIES AND FRIENDS BITTERLY DIVIDED.

THO AT FIRST WE WERE QUITE HAPPY, CERTAIN DIFFICULTIES SOON AROSE.

SHE INSISTED UPON STAYING OUT ALL NIGHT...

AND BROUGHT HOME THE MANGLED CARCASSES OF SMALL ANIMALS.

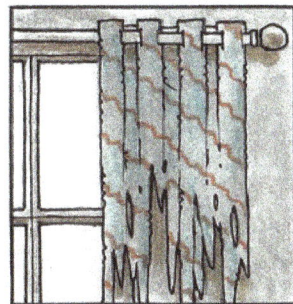
EPISODES OF DESTRUCTIVE BEHAVIOR SHE WOULD DISMISS AS NO BIG DEAL.

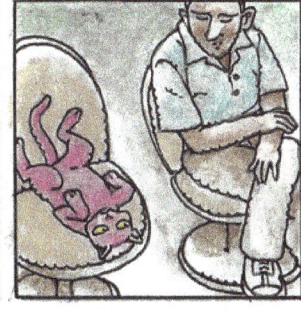
WE SPENT MANY HOURS IN THERAPY.

TOO MANY COUPLES SPLIT UP THESE DAYS OVER MINOR DISAGREEMENTS.

OUR FIRST LITTER IS ON THE WAY!

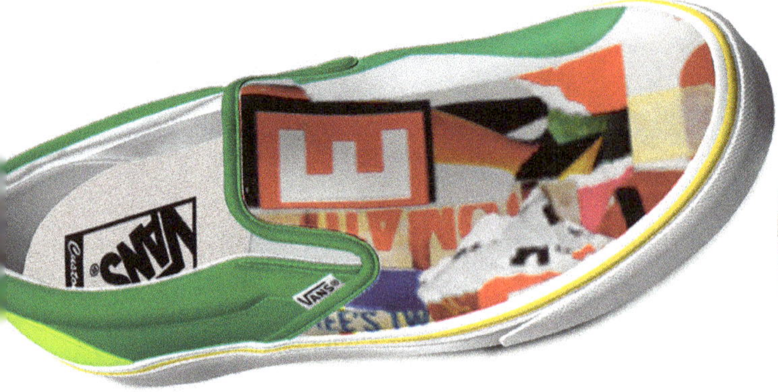

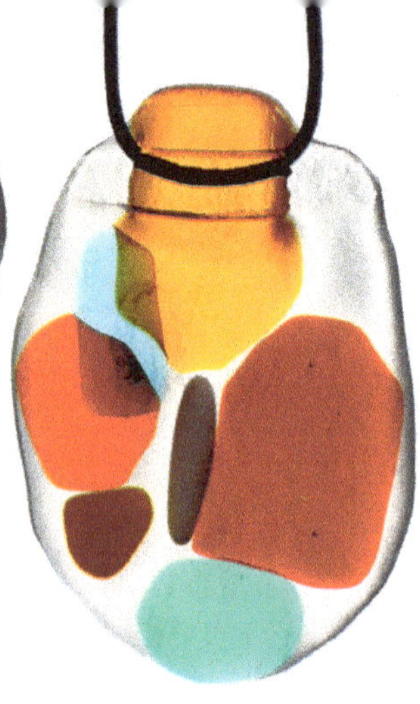

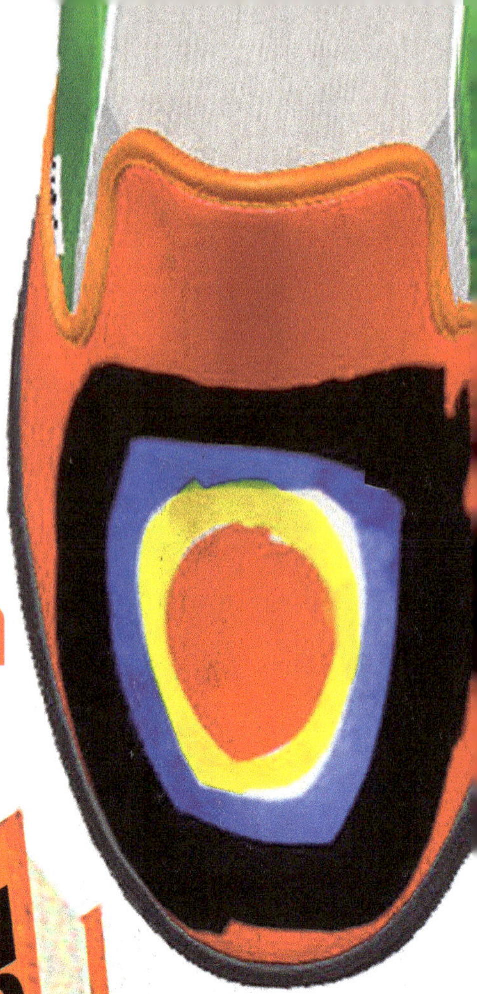

visit
www.rosenworld.com
for
Sneakers, Signed Books,
Melty Jewels
and Original Artwork
by Laurie Rosenwald, First Pancake,
Occasional Swede
& America's
Favorite Bystander

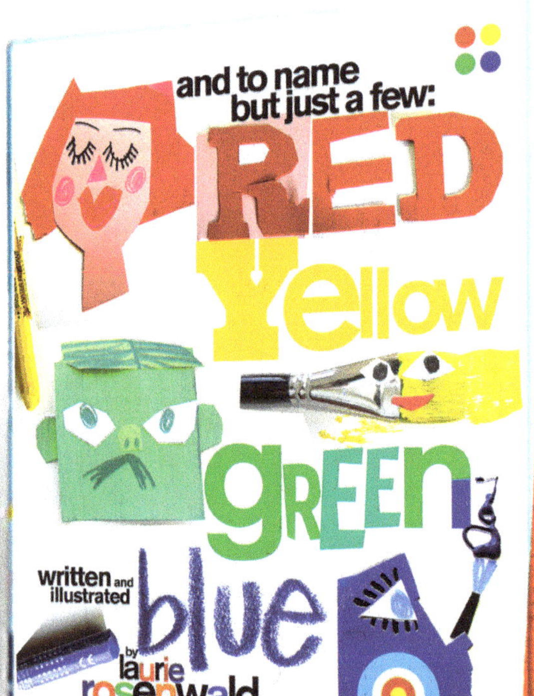
and to name but just a few:
RED
Yellow
green
blue
written and illustrated by laurie rosenwald

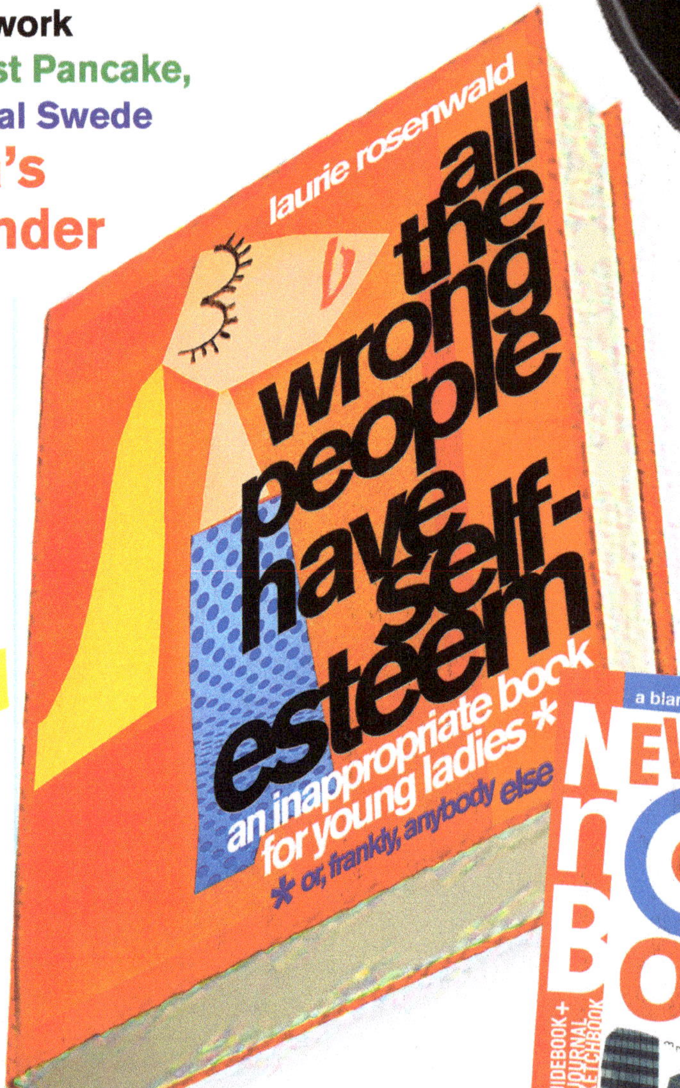
laurie rosenwald
all the wrong people have self-esteem
an inappropriate book for young ladies *
* or, frankly, anybody else

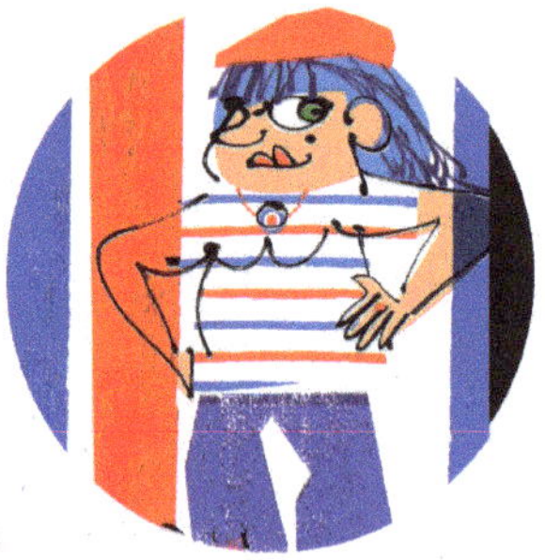

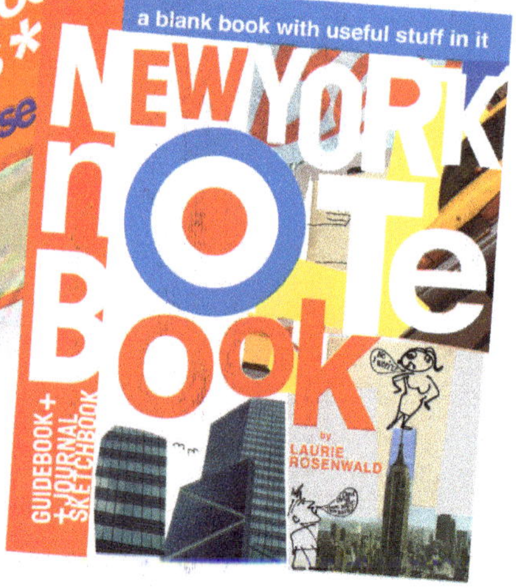
a blank book with useful stuff in it
NEW YORK NOTE BOOK
GUIDEBOOK + JOURNAL + SKETCHBOOK
by LAURIE ROSENWALD

"Laurie's voice is fresh sounding, funny, and completely her own." -David Sedaris

OUR BACK PAGES

WHAT AM I DOING HERE?

Welcome to the Catskills, home of Jack E. "Jack" Jackie • By Mike Reiss

Desperation Vacation

My wife has dragged me like a piece of battered luggage to over 130 countries, most recently the –stans: Paki-, Kazakh-, and Uzbeki-. She was planning a trip to Afghani-, for reasons I don't quite under-, when the pandemic hit. Suddenly we were stranded, unable to leave the tiny island home we call Manhattan. Since we had no car and were leery of using public transit, we were limited by how far we could walk in a day. Like medieval villagers, we never went more than five miles from home.

For me, it was a dream version of New York: no crowds, no noise, no Broadway musicals. After four months of this, my wife wanted OUT, but no one would take us; Americans were considered too disease-ridden to be allowed into any country. I wasn't afraid of Afghanistan—they were afraid of me. To call us lepers is an insult to leprosy—it's nowhere near as contagious as Covid-19.

In desperation, my wife and I did what New Yorkers have done for centuries to leave town for the summer—we went to the Catskills. I'd only been there once, half a century ago. As a kid growing up in Connecticut, I saw commercials for the Catskill Game Farm every three or four minutes. The ads featured Roland Lindemann, owner of America's only private zoo, who talked like one of the cuter Nazis on *Hogan's Heroes*. I nagged my father to take me there—it was a

MIKE REISS is Intrepid Traveler for *The American Bystander*.

A monument to Old Forgettable himself, President Martin Van Buren.

hundred miles from our home, but Dad acted like I'd asked him to pull me by rickshaw to the moon. It was worth all the begging; the Catskill Game Farm was a magical place, even better than the commercials. And a llama spit at my father.

The Catskills are 6,000 square miles of mountains, rivers, lakes and mosquitoes just two hours outside of NYC. Americans were introduced to the area by Washington Irving's 1819 story "Rip Van Winkle." It's the tale of a truly American hero, a lazy guy who gets drunk, goes bowling, and then sleeps really, really late. (The story posits that thunder is caused by little men bowling in the mountains. There is near-constant thunder in the Catskills, even on sunny days, and it does sound just like a bowling alley, so I'm on board with this theory.) Two centuries after the story's publication, you can go to the Catskills and rent an ATV from Rip Van Winkle Sports, gas it up at Rip Van Winkle Service Station, ride it to Rip Van Winkle Vineyard and then drunk drive into Rip Van Winkle Lake. Quite a legacy for a hero whose only superpower was napping.

The only other thing the area is famous for is the Catskills resorts: Grossinger's, Brown's, Kutsher's, The Concord. All of these catered to people who loved being outdoors as long as it didn't involve doing anything (we're called Jews); the most dangerous sport they indulged in all summer was tanning. These resorts also launched the careers of a generation of comedians, including Woody Allen, Allan Sherman, Jackie Mason, Jackie Vernon, Jackie Allen, Vernon Sherman, Sherman Vernon, and Jack E. "Jack" Jackie.

All of these resorts are defunct, either torn down or in serious decay. The closest thing standing is Scott's Oquage Lake House Resort, which doubled for a Catskills resort in *The Marvelous Mrs. Maisel*, but even that was shut down for Covid-19. Everything was closed for Covid-19. There was absolutely nothing to do in the Catskills and my wife had just booked us a week there.

Hotels are different during a pandemic: there's no breakfast, no food of any kind, and no maid service. Your room just gets messier and messier as the days pass. It's like staying in the guest room of a friend who doesn't really like you.

We were in a lovely place called the Hotel Vienna, run by a sweet man named Prick. I'm sure this wasn't his name, but I asked him three times, and it kept sounding like Prick. It was part of a bigger problem: Prick seemed to mumble the key word in every sentence:

"Anything you need, anything at all, just dial nine-three-*shnopp*."

"For the best pizza you ever had in your life, go to *Shnxvolz*'s on *Gllzbmph* Road."

"If you touch the *shmorsh* in your room, it might kill you."

The top tourist attraction in the region is Olana, the home of painter Frederic Edwin Church. Church's bill-

Explore the world's largest cartoon database

Over **500,000** cartoons from the
Bystander, **New Yorker** & more

CAR**T**OONCOLLECTIONS.COM

board-sized canvases pad out the collections of American art museums. Olana is a gorgeous estate and as fake as Disneyland; the surrounding woodland was designed and planted by Church to look like 'real' nature.

Another piece of *faux* Americana is Woodstock, a hippy-dippy town coasting off a concert that took place fifty years ago and forty miles away. Calling Woodstock home to the Woodstock Festival is like calling Trenton the Big Apple.

For more historic mislabeling, visit "Pratt Rock—America's Mount Rushmore." (I thought *Mount Rushmore* was America's Mount Rushmore.) Zaddock Pratt was a successful tanner, banker, and Congressman who named everything he saw after himself: Pratt Rock is in Prattsville, downriver from Pratt Falls (whose slippery rocks actually cause many pratfalls).

If you're interested in Martin Van Buren, and nobody is (including, possibly, Mrs. Van Buren), you can visit his birth site, the home he retired to, and his grave in under a half hour. They're all contained within a two-mile radius—he didn't get around much. As eighth President of the United States, Van Buren is best remembered for his many colorful nicknames: "Old Kinderhook," "Sly Fox," "The Little Magician," "Mr. Forgettable," and "Really—You Were President?"

We had a week of wonder and weirdness, but there was one last place I had to visit: the Catskill Game Farm. As a child, I whined till my Dad drove me there. Now that I was a man, I could whine until my wife took me.

We arrived at the zoo to find it had been closed since 2006; there was a creepy rumor that all the animals had been sold to exotic meat butchers. But I had hope—the buildings and enclosures were still around, slowly crumbling away. Nostalgia freaks, aging Boomers and fans of decay were allowed to tour the facilities two days a month...but we'd come too late.

"Maybe we can sneak in," said my wife, standing right next to a sign reading "YOU CANNOT SNEAK IN." (That's not a joke—it was the most explicit sign I'd ever read: "THESE PREMISES ARE MONITORED BY SECURITY CAMERAS 24 HOURS A DAY. IF YOU SNEAK IN POLICE WILL CATCH YOU AND PUT YOU IN JAIL.")

My wife seemed to see some wiggle room in these words. As a gardener left the grounds, the electric gate remained open just long enough for my wife to squeeze our rented Jeep through. She was like Clark Griswold, the lead character in Chevy Chase's only good film, *Vacation*—she'd brought us to the Catskills for an adventure and, dammit, we were going to have one. She'd found a little slice of Afghanistan in southeastern New York. We roared past signs reading "NO VEHICLES EVER" and "YOU ARE BREAKING THE LAW," our Jeep bouncing over dirt roads and gravel paths too rugged for the movie *Sorcerer*. And you know, I loved it. The fences had fallen, the cages were overgrown with weeds, the roofs of enclosures had caved in...but I could still see the Catskill Game Farm of my youth. It hadn't aged gracefully, but then neither had I.

If you ever visit the Catskills, check out the Old Game Farm. (Try to do it legally.) There are two other spots not to be missed: the breath-taking Kaaterskill Falls and Art Omi, a 120-acre sculpture garden. There's no joke here—I don't have to crap on everything. Jesus, you people.

OUR BACK PAGES

P.S. MUELLER THINKS LIKE THIS
The cartoonist/broadcaster/writer is always walking around, looking at stuff • By P.S. Mueller

"He comes up for the summer."

Greasy Bees

By 2022, Apple was floating on a sea of trillions. Then they began upgrading.

First, summer was rechristened "Shiny Bang," which it remained until June of 2022. Delayed by a maddeningly random series of glitches, Apple ended up just slapping the number "2" on the season and hoping for the best.

Sparrows around the world exploded. Climate scientists and ornithologists everywhere agreed that all was not well. But so it remained, for then.

Then, Angus Jobs stepped in. He'd won control of Apple following an expensive visit to the Supreme Court's secret headquarters in Bottineau, North Dakota.

A distant relative, Angus Jobs had a maniacal hatred of sameness. Also, he had a birthmark shaped like a huge cornflake. It was the color of a fine claret and he assiduously avoided Bordeaux vines.

After his victory, Angus J. owned most of everything: Subway sandwich locations, beach equipment, half of the Rocky Mountains, even Sarah Lee confections, as well as a dozen renegade A&W Root Beer franchises that escaped to Greenland.

He owned the Dollar Stores, too, by the way! A guy like that could really DO a lot of stuff. He could end the sameness.

Anyway, the debut of "2" proved to be an expensive undertaking as the cost of replacing several billion sparrows had been underestimated. Sand had to be brought in from the Gobi desert, now owned and operated by Bill Gates.

(Gates, by the way, is nesting in the golden afterlife chamber at the center of the "sand-style" pyramid out there on Route 70. Devoured by a black hole, Elon Musk literally got nothing.)

After fixing the birds, Angus Jobs put his right hand in and he put his right hand out, and that was the end of "2" sameness. Summer was now "The Big Shiny"…but it was *still* too predictable. No pending updates. *Nothing*.

So Angus sent a team of people to rouse retired president Donald J. Trump from his soporific state, and chase away the greasy bees that seemed to adore him so. These Trumpers were the stingless drones, long since cast out; their god was covered with thousands of large and harmless male bees, soaked with hive lube and rolled in cracker crumbs. The ex-president occasionally snorted and snacked on a handful of drones. A special injection was given, and Trump moved, pawing away the bees suckling at his eyelids. Then he sat up and flashed that look of his around his cell and asked, "When's tee time? And who is this Bezos guy?"

At that precise moment, suction bombs planted around his base exploded, and Trump was thrown back onto a soft bed of confused and groggy bees.

In the distance, a speck appeared. It blurred and whirled and shuddered close, landing in the enormous, almost night-like shadow of the former president. It was a huge Amazon drone.

A hatch opened, and reality mogul Jeff Bezos stepped out onto the Gobi sand…with a titanium golf club.

The sameness was about to end.

P.S. MUELLER is Staff Liar of *The American Bystander*.

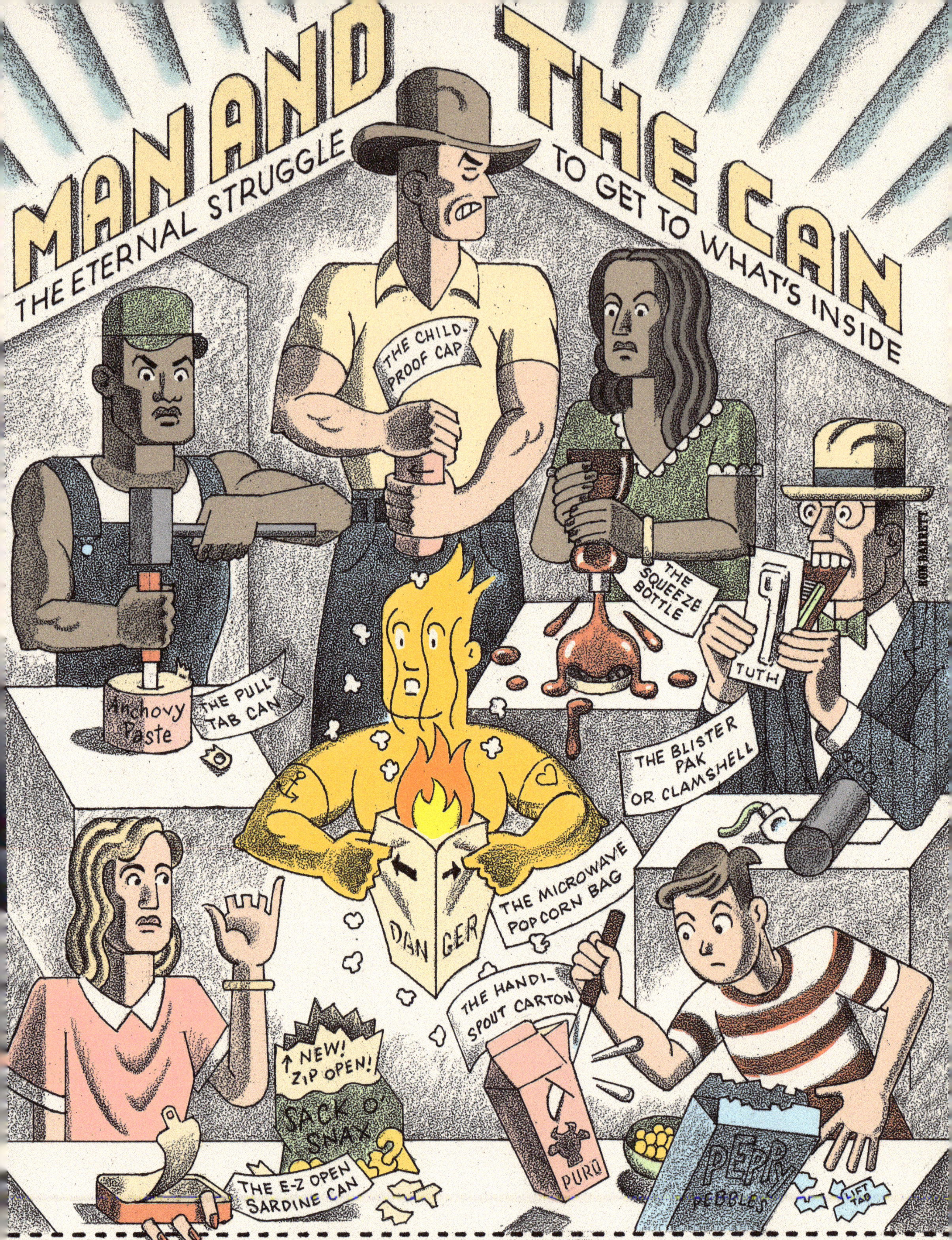
MAN AND THE CAN
THE ETERNAL STRUGGLE TO GET TO WHAT'S INSIDE
THE CHILD-PROOF CAP
THE SQUEEZE BOTTLE
TUTH
THE BLISTER PAK OR CLAMSHELL
Anchovy Paste
THE PULL-TAB CAN
THE MICROWAVE POPCORN BAG
DAN GER
THE HANDI-SPOUT CARTON
↑ NEW! ZIP OPEN!
SACK O SNAX
THE E-Z OPEN SARDINE CAN
PURO
PEPPY PEBBLES
LIFT TAB

CUT ALONG DOTTED LINE TO ACCESS PREVIOUS PAGE

www.ingramcontent.com/pod-product-compliance
Lightning Source LLC
Chambersburg PA
CBHW061755290426
44108CB00029B/3001